The Geopolitics of Cyberspace: a Diplomatic Perspective

Diplomacy and Foreign Policy

Volumes published in this Brill Research Perspective are listed at *brill.com/rpdf*

The Geopolitics of Cyberspace: a Diplomatic Perspective

By

Shaun Riordan

BRILL

LEIDEN | BOSTON

This paperback book edition is simultaneously published as issue 3.3 (2018) of *Diplomacy and Foreign Policy*, DOI:10.1163/24056006-12340011.

Library of Congress Control Number: 2019942160

Typeface for the Latin, Greek, and Cyrillic scripts: "Brill". See and download: brill.com/brill-typeface.

ISBN 978-90-04-40936-1 (paperback)
ISBN 978-90-04-40937-8 (e-book)

This book is printed on acid-free paper and produced in a sustainable manner.

Contents

The Geopolitics of Cyberspace: a Diplomatic Perspective

Shaun Riordan
European Institute of International Studies, Salamanca, Spain
Shaun.riordan@ieeiweb.eu

Abstract

The Internet has been seen as the harbinger of a world without borders or sovereignty. But states have recently reemerged in Cyberspace, asserting sovereignty or using it to pursue conflict with rivals. This article explores the geopolitics of Cyberspace. It argues that critical geopolitical concepts like geopolitical fields, culture and conditions can offer insights into the behaviour of actors in Cyberspace. The argument is explored through case studies of the US, Russia and China. The article goes beyond traditional nation states to apply similar analysis to the European Union and Internet companies. It concludes that both classical and critical geopolitics can make valuable contributions to the analysis of Cyberspace, and the behaviour of both state and non-state actors. Diplomacy has a crucial role in managing geopolitical conflicts in Cyberspace. But diplomats need to rethink their engagement and reform the structures and cultures in which they operate.

Keywords

geopolitics – Cyberspace – Internet – cybersecurity – diplomacy – international relations – international law – cyberwar – cyberconflict – cyberdiplomacy

Supplementary materials including a slide presentation and a video prepared by the author can be accessed at https://brill.figshare.com/s/ca58dfdd9f109f7683b6

•••

 | DOI:10.1163/9789004409378_002

> … thinking is also research. My book reflects the limitations of an attempt to deal with a large and complex subject simply by thinking it through.
>
> HEDLEY BULL

∵

1 Introduction

The Internet was supposed to overcome all borders to generate a new networked world, where nations and their Governments would matter less. Civil society would talk to directly to civil society. Foreign Ministries and diplomats would slowly disappear. Instead of the old agendas centred around the balance of power and competition for territory and resources, the debates mediated through global online networks would focus on the existential challenges confronting mankind: climate change, pandemic disease, poverty etc. This anti-Governmental aspect was captured by ICANN (the Internet Corporation for Assigned Names and Numbers), a not-for-profit company registered in California responsible for a large part of Internet governance.

It has not turned out like that. Reports of cyber attacks against major corporations are an almost daily event. Governments and their surrogates are continually launching disruption, espionage and online disinformation operations against each other. Degeneration operations with Kinetic effects – causing physical damage and/or injuries – are so far rarer, but there is at least one example. Citizens are increasingly concerned about the use to which their data is being put by Internet companies, and the extent of surveillance by their Governments. Online disinformation campaigns are blamed for influencing the Brexit referendum in the UK and the Presidential election in the US. Internet governance has become a hotly contested political issue, with Governments divided between those who support the existing multistakeholder model (the "Free Internet Countries") and those who advocate bringing Internet governance within the UN or other inter-Governmental institutions (the "Cyber Sovereignty Advocates"). At least one author[1] has spoken about a new cold war in Cyberspace.

With this resurgence of the state, Cyberspace is beginning to look ever more like physical space, with similar challenges (although, fortunately, without similar levels of violence and bloodshed, at least so far). There are two further

1 Alexander Klimburg: *The Darkening Web: The War for Cyberspace*, Penguin, 2017.

differences relevant to this article. Diplomats have largely ignored Cyberspace as a domain for diplomatic activity. They have focused instead on the tools which Cyberspace can offer for carrying out their tasks, whether messenger apps in multinational negotiations or social media platforms for consular work or public diplomacy. They have left Internet governance and, even more so, cybersecurity to technicians, communications experts and the military/intelligence services. The second difference is that there is little if any international law in Cyberspace (former NSA and CIA director Michael Hayden has said that there is no law in Cyberspace[2]). The conventions that have been agreed (eg Budapest) have not been ratified by key actors in Cyberspace. There is no universal agreement about whether international law applies in Cyberspace. International law in physical space is limited and imperfectly honoured. But there is a broad agreement on what it is and how it should be applied.

This article seeks to explore three questions: if Cyberspace is developing in similar ways to physical space, can the concept of geopolitics be applied to it? If so, can geopolitical analysis help differentiate between the activities and motivations of different actors in Cyberspace, as well as understand how their activities in Cyberspace relate to their activities in physical space? And what are the implications for diplomacy and foreign policy?

The article begins by exploring the concept of geopolitics. Twenty years ago the term was hardly ever heard. Its association with German Geopolitik theories in the Weimar republic, and their influence on Nazi concepts like Lebensraum, left it tainted. Even in its Anglo-Saxon form, it was seen as promoting an excessive geographical determinism. Today the term is thrown around with cheery abandon. It is used by political consultancy and security companies, as well as journalists. Its indiscriminate use risks emptying it of content (rather as the indiscriminate use of "diplomacy" risks the same). This article will seek to recover some rigour in the use of the term. It will do so in two ways. First it will explore whether classical geopolitics, the idea that politics and geography interact to shape (not determine) international events, is applicable to Cyberspace. At first sight, this appears absurd, as Cyberspace almost by definition has no geography. But the article will explore to what extent the structures of Cyberspace impact on the behaviour of actors in the way that physical geographies do in physical space.

Secondly the article will use concepts from Critical Geopolitics to explore the behaviour of individual actors. It will examine whether the way in which actors experience the Internet (geopolitical condition) and their geopolitical culture combine to shape their behaviour in the different geopolitical fields

2 Klimburg: *The Darkening Web*.

in which they operate in Cyberspace. This analysis is applied to three state actors, the US, Russia and China. These are chosen not only because they are major players in Cyberspace, but also because they have different experiences of the Internet and represent three different ways of behaving in Cyberspace: enforcement, disruption and espionage. The European Union is not a nation state and has limited cyber offence capacities. But it has sought to play a leading role in regulation of Cyberspace, in particular data protection, where it aspires to impose global norms. The article analyses to what extent this reflects the EU's experience of Cyberspace and its own, post-modern, geopolitical culture. Finally, the article applies the same analysis to Internet companies, and especially search engines and social media companies. They do not see themselves as geopolitical actors, but they increasingly shape events in Cyberspace and serve as the geopolitical fields where cyber disinformation conflicts are fought out.

The last part of the article explores the implications of this analysis for foreign policy and diplomacy. It seeks to maintain a distinction between statecraft, foreign policy and diplomacy (a distinction rarely made – Kissinger's magnus opus "Diplomacy"[3] is almost entirely about statecraft, with diplomacy itself rarely raising its head). In particular, it considers how the geopolitical analysis in the previous sections can help diplomats identify the motivations and intentions of actors in Cyberspace, as well as common ground on which agreements might be constructed on norms of behaviour in Cyberspace. It also considers how the concept of "Tech Ambassador", introduced by the Danish Government with the appointment of an Ambassador to the technology sector, might be expanded to engage with Internet companies about their geopolitical responsibilities.

This article does not seek to be definitive but rather a preliminary exploration of the relevance of the concept of "geopolitics" in the analysis of Cyberspace, and the extent to which is can support diplomats in their efforts to manage the challenges of this new domain. As Kello[4] argues, international relations studies have been slow to get to grips with Cyberspace, which both international relations scholars and diplomats have tended to leave to the technicians. But as Clemenceau once said, war is too important to be left to generals, and Cyberspace is too important to be left to technicians. To the extent to which Cyberspace and physical space interact with each other, and become interdependent on each other, we need to develop non-technical ways of engaging with Cyberspace. This article argues that geopolitical analysis may offer one possible framework.

3 Henry Kissinger: *Diplomacy*, Simon and Schuster, 1994.
4 Lucas Kello: *The Virtual Weapon and World Order*, Yale University Press, 2017.

2 Geopolitics

The terms "geopolitics" and "geopolitical" are now almost ubiquitous in debates about international relations. This was not true twenty years ago, when the concept of geopolitics was seen as intellectually suspect and, for some, unacceptably linked to the ideology of the Third Reich through such practitioners as Karl Haushofer. At the same time, the high point of globalisation and America's unipolar moment[5] suggested that the kind of "geopolitical" agendas associated with inter-state conflict were something of the past. Fukuyama[6] had written of the End of History, implying a world in which all states and cultures would progressively converge on the liberal market model. Cooper[7] held up the European Union as the model of the "post-modern" state, where sovereignty was shared rather than defended and conflict replaced by dialogue. The European Union's norm-based diplomacy was based on the attractiveness of this "post-modern" state (and its economic success).

Thus the return of the term "geopolitics" can to some extent be seen as a mark of disillusion with this millenarian optimism. As Kagan[8] put it, "The world has become normal again". Geopolitics and geopolitical have become code for a realist view of the world that eschews both the liberalism and neo-conservatism that held sway either side of the millennium. Geopolitical risk has entered the everyday discourse of major corporations as well as Governments. Geopolitical risk consultancy companies have multiplied as "geopolitical uncertainty" increases, offering to anticipate international events for their clients, and protect them from the worst of their impact. Many of these companies are headed up "geopolitical gurus", like George Friedman and Ian Bremmer, who hold forth in the media (and social media) about the implications of international events or international trends, and write books with titles like "The Next Hundred Years" and "The End of the Free Market".[9] A leading figure in this revival of geopolitics has been Robert Kaplan, the title of whose book "The Revenge of Geography: What the Map Tells us About Coming Conflicts and the Battle Against Fate" leaves little doubt about his intentions.[10]

---

5 Hal Brands: *Making the Unipolar Moment: US Foreign Policy and the Rise of the Post-Cold War Order*, Cornell, 2016.

6 Francis Fukuyama: *The End of History and the Last Man*, Simon and Schuster, 2006.

7 Robert Cooper: *The Breaking of Nations: Order and Chaos in the Twenty-First Century*, Atlantic Books, 2003.

8 Robert Kagan: *The Return of History and the End of Dreams*, Atlantic Books, 2008.

9 George Friedman: *The Next 100 Years: A Forecast for the 21st Century*, Allison & Busby, 2010; Ian Bremmer: *The End of the Freemarket: Who Wins the War between States and Corporations?*, Viking, 2010.

10 Robert D Kaplan: *The Revenge of Geography: What the Map Can Tell Us About Coming Conflicts and the Battle Against Fate*, Random House, 2013.

There are two problems with this sudden renewed enthusiasm for geopolitics. Firstly, it risks concealing the return of a crude form of geopolitical determinism. There is a tendency to argue that certain features of physical and political geography reflect eternal verities about the human situation, and that these predict where conflict will inevitably break out in the future, as it has in the past. "Prisoners of Geography: Ten Maps That Tell You Everything You Need to Know About Global Politics" by the journalist Tim Marshall is a best-selling example, as is Kagan's "The Return of Marco Polo's World".[11] The influence of these books is increased both by the realist element of this kind of geopolitical discourse – after a period of idealism it's time to get real about the world – but also by the implication that geopolitics can reveal concealed truths about the world. Geopolitics, and geopolitical writers, can serve as a guide to what is really going on behind international events and what is likely to happen in the future. An example of this is the forthcoming "How They Rule the World: the Secret Strategies of World Power" by Spanish geopolitician Pedro Baños.[12] Geopolitical discourse risks morphing into conspiracy theory.

The second problem is that the over-extended and indiscriminate use of the terms geopolitics and geopolitical risk emptying them of meaning. A similar process has happened with the term "diplomacy".[13] Scholars, and to some extent practitioners, in recent years have enthusiastically proposed a host of new "diplomacies", ranging from public and digital diplomacy to sports, science or even gastro diplomacy. In doing so they have implied an even greater host of "new diplomats", who carry out these various forms of diplomacy. The problem is that amongst all this creativity, the concept of diplomacy itself, in as far as it relates to what diplomats do (and have done) gets lost. The concept of diplomacy is hollowed out. If everything is diplomacy, and everyone is a diplomat, then nothing is, and no-one is. A similar process is happening with geopolitics. The point can be made by thinking about the term geopolitical risk. As we have seen, this is bandied around board rooms, and consulting companies make considerable sums claiming to be able to analyse, anticipate and mitigate it. But most of the risks these consultancies analyse are not geopolitical in the strict sense of the word. Rather they are political, social, legislative or technological risks. Even risks that might reasonably be termed geopolitical – for example inter-state conflict, the imposition of sanctions regimes, trade wars – might more accurately be described as international risk.

---

11 Tim Marshall: *Prisoners of Geography: Ten Maps that Tell You Everything You Need to Know About Global Politics*, Elliott and Thompson, 2015.
Robert D Kaplan: *The Return of Marco Polo's World*, Random House, 2018.

12 Pedro Baños: *How They Rule the World*, Random House, 2019.

13 Shaun Riordan: *Stop Inventing New Diplomacies*, https://www.uscpublicdiplomacy.org/blog/stop-inventing-new-diplomacies.

"Geopolitical risk" has, for both the consulting companies and their clients, become a convenient catch-all for all the non-commercial risks a company may confront in its international operations.[14] Given this, it is increasingly unclear what geopolitical means, or whether it means anything other than a realist approach to international affairs. In other words, the current popularity of geopolitics may be reducing the term to a crude geographic determinism, with an accompanying fatalism about the prospects of conflict in certain geographical zones, or a way of talking about international affairs in a period of instability and uncertainty.

Both possibilities pose problems for this article. If geopolitics is a crude geographical determinism, reflecting eternal verities about where human conflicts arise, it is difficult to see how it could be applied to Cyberspace. At most, Cyberspace could become a domain in which the inevitable conflicts arising from geopolitical verities would be fought out. But that would not amount to a geopolitics of Cyberspace. Equally, if geopolitics has been hollowed out as a concept to the extent that it is little more than a catch-all for risk analysts or a certain way of talking about international affairs, it is difficult to talk about a geopolitics of Cyberspace, other than in an equally hollowed out way. A realist approach to cybersecurity, for example. But this article wants to explore if there is a geopolitics of Cyberspace, parallel to but different from the geopolitics of physical space, and if so, what are the implications for diplomats. To do so it will adopt two approaches to geopolitics. Firstly it will try to recover or reconstruct the classical geopolitics from the beginning of the last century. It will explore whether this essentially physical approach can be applied to the structures of Cyberspace. Secondly it will engage with critical geopolitics and in particular concepts like the geopolitical field[15] and diplomatic assemblage.[16] It will not only consider how they can be applied to Cyberspace, but also the extent to which they can help us understand the behaviour of major state and non-state actors.

3 Classical Geopolitics

In some senses the origins of geopolitics lie in a disagreement between a US navy officer and a British academic. Mahan was an historian and a US naval

14 Kesteleyn, Riordan and Ruël: *Introduction: Business Diplomacy*, Hague Journal of Diplomacy, Vol 9, No 4 (2014).

15 Gerard Toal: *Near Abroad: Putin, the West, and the Contest over Ukraine and the Caucasus*, Oxford University Press, 2017.

16 Jason Dittmer: *Diplomatic Material: Affect, Assemblage and Foreign Policy*, Duke University Press, 2017.

captain. In the Influence of Sea Power upon History 1660-1873, Mahan[17] argued that the key to a country's economic and political success on the world stage lay in the domination of global sea lanes. Building on his own studies of British naval and imperial success, he maintained that maritime power would determine national greatness in the future as it has in the past. The sea was a "great common" on which countries could project power through unseen lines of power between strategically located strongpoints, as did Britain's Royal Navy on sea routes between a global network of naval bases and coaling stations.

Given Mahan's admiration for the Royal Navy, it is ironic that his concept of geopolitics was opposed by a British academic. Mackinder was a geographer and Director of the London School of Economics. Mackinder was not only interested in geography, and how it shaped international relations, but also how new technologies impacted on both geography and international relations, particularly the railways and telegraph. With imperial exploration and expansion drawing to a close Mackinder[18] saw the world as a completed and now closed political system. Rather than the sea lanes he concentrated on the central Asian land mass, arguing that its resources and internal lines of communication would give it the advantage in future inter-state competition. Prior to the First World War he referred to this as the "geographical pivot of history" and after as the "Heartland". His most famous aphorism was "Who rules East-Europe commands the Heartland; who rules the Heartland commands the World-Island; who rules the World-Island controls the world". In particular he was concerned that the Heartland was inaccessible to naval power, which would mean the inevitable diminution of the British Imperial Power if any one power, or alliance of powers, were to gain control of the Heartland. Later in the 1940s, the Dutch-American international relations theorist Spykman refined Mackinder's theory.[19] Spykman accepted the Heartland, but argued that it was surrounded by an unstable rimland, running through eastern Europe, the Middle East and Southern and Eastern Asia. Spykman suggested that conflict for control of the Heartland tended to be fought out in this rimland rather than in the Heartland itself. Countries outside this rimland tended to be more stable.

Prior to the First World War Mahan's ideas were more popular. But after the War, Mackinder's thinking was taken up, especially in Germany, where

17 A T Mahan: *The Influence of Sea Power Upon History 1660-1783*, Dover, 2012.

18 Halford John Mackinder: *Democratic Ideals and Reality & The Geographical Pivot of History*, Origami Books, 2018.

19 Nicholas J Spykman: *America's Strategy in World Politics: The United States and the Balance of Power*, Transaction Publishers, 2007.

scholars and statesmen sought reasons for Germany's defeat and pointers towards the path to recovery. Geopolitics became a subject studied in universities. Geopoliticians and Geopolitics Institutes, both as university departments and think-tanks, flourished.[20] For our purposes we can focus on the most controversial, Karl Haushofer. Haushofer was a former officer in the Bavarian army who taught political geography at the University of Munich. He combined the ideas of Mackinder with those of the Swedish political scientist Kjellén (who taught that the state was a geographic organism or life form) and the German political geographer Ratzel (who introduced Darwinian competition to the organic concept of the state).[21] Kjellén also argued that geopolitics should be seen not just as an area of academic study, but as a science offering concrete recommendations for state policy and behaviour (echoes of Bremmer and Friedman?). From these influences, Haushofer produced his own version of Geopolitics as a science. His novelties included the concept of *Lebensraum* (living space for the German people) and autarchy, freeing Germany from dependence on trade with other, potentially hostile, powers. He recommended an alliance between Germany, Russia and Japan to control the Heartland as the only means of resisting the Anglo-Saxon maritime powers the UK and the US.[22] Haushofer is significant because of his relations to Hitler and his deputy Heß. Heß was Haushofer's student at the University of Munich and through him, and some direct contact with Hitler himself, he may have influenced the geopolitical passages in Mein Kampf. This influence can be exaggerated (as it was in post-war reports on Haushofer's responsibility for war crimes). As Murphy points out,[23] the halcyon days of geopolitics were the Weimar Republic; once the Nazis were in power, geopolitical recipes were abandoned for Hitler's racist and anti-Bolshevik obsessions. Nevertheless the damage was done to the reputation of geopolitics, which all but disappeared until rescued in recent years by the disillusion with globalisation and the realisation that the world is not flat.

At first sight it would seem that Classical Geopolitics has little to offer in the analysis of Cyberspace. It is focused so firmly on the consequences of geographical features for politics that it actually says very little about politics itself. Cyberspace, being virtual, does not have physical geographical features which can impact on the way in which politics and political objectives are pursued on its networks. However, the reference to the networks of Cyberspace

20 David T Murphy: *The Heroic Earth: Geopolitical Thought in Weimar Germany, 1918-1933*, Kent State University, 1997.

21 David T Murphy: *The Heroic Earth.*

22 Holger H Herwig: *The Demon of Geopolitics: How Karl Haushofer "Educated" Hitler and Hess*, Rowan and Littlefield, 2016.

23 David T Murphy: *The Heroic Earth.*

does offer a clue about how even Classical Geopolitics might be relevant to Cyberspace. Despite its geographical determinism, there are several respects in which Classical Geopolitics might be relevant to an analysis of Cyberspace. Abstracting from the actual geographical features Classical Geopolitics focuses on structures, and how structures influence and constrain the decisions taken by political actors, whether thought of in terms of states or the individual statesmen within those states. In a sense it offers a structural analysis of international relations. As we will see, Cyberspace also has structures, both in terms of the physical structures of cables and processing centres which underlie it and in terms of the networks on which its data is carried. Some of these structures have developed with the Internet, others have been deliberately designed and positioned by state or non-state actors. These structures influence and constrain actions which Internet users can take. The second interesting feature is Mackinder's focus on how new technologies (in his case the railway and telegraph) can change the geopolitical calculation. This chimes with the discussions today about how new digital technologies are changing (and have changed) international relations and the ways in which they are managed. In other words, there is a debate not only about the geopolitics of Cyberspace, but also about how Cyberspace (and other disruptive technologies like machine learning AI and blockchain) are changing geopolitics. Finally, although Kjellén's and Haushofer's conception of the state as an organic being has uncomfortably Spenglerian[24] overtones (not to mention authoritarian ones) it does at least capture the idea of the dynamism and evolution of the different geopolitical actors in relation to one another. A feature of digital technologies is the extent to which they have facilitated the participation of a broad range of non-state actors in international affairs, from companies to NGOs and civil society actors. Any geopolitics of Cyberspace will need to take account of the role of these non-state actors, just as the geopolitics of the 18th century had to take account of the British East India Company and the Anti-Slavery League. A geopolitics of Cyberspace must move beyond the state to look at non-state actors, including both Internet companies and non-state hackers to consider how they evolve in relation to each other and state actors. This will be particularly relevant to the Internet companies.

4 Critical Geopolitics

However, Classical Geopolitics retains its geographic determinism, which limits its relevance. Franco-German relations demonstrate the problem. The

24 Oswald Spengler: *The Decline of the West*, Blurb Books, 2018.

geography of the Franco-German border has not changed since the late 1930s. But the political relationship has changed entirely. There remains a degree of rivalry between Paris and Berlin, but it is now expressed in debates about the future of the European Union. In other words, although geography is relevant in international relations, it is not determinant. Politics (and other factors) affects what that geography means, and this can change over time. This has led to the development of critical geopolitics, which in a sense tries to put the politics back into geopolitics. Some critical geopolitics scholars argue that critical geopolitics is to geopolitics as literary criticism is to literature.[25] Critical geopolitics not only criticises the geographical determinism of classical geopolitics, but also the way in which it neutralises the prejudices which lie behind the interpretation of geographical features: converting nationalist or racial prejudices into "scientific" and "inevitable" facts.

Toal[26] identifies three concepts in critical geopolitics which will be useful in the analysis of geopolitics in Cyberspace: the geopolitical field, geopolitical cultures and the geopolitical condition. Geopolitical fields[27] explore how power structures like states and markets have produced spaces, territories and landscapes, environments and social agents. Toal defines a geopolitical field as both the sociospatial context of statecraft and the social players, roles and spatial dynamics constituting the arena. In terms of Cyberspace, this concept allows us to explore how the different state and non-state actors interact with each other and how this gives meanings to the structures of Cyberspace. Important here is not only the role the different actors play, but the role they think they are playing, and how that affects policy decisions.

This feeds into Toal's second concept, geopolitical culture. According to Toal,[28] a state's spatial identity and the ongoing debate about it, defines its geopolitical culture. In Cyberspace, this culture is defined by the way states think about Cyberspace and the Internet and the place they see themselves holding in it, as well as the role they believe they are playing. This influences not only whether a state actively seeks to penetrate foreign Internet systems (and whether it does so covertly or openly) but also what kind of penetration it commits: cyber armed attack, cyber disruption or cyberespionage. This applies to non-state actors as well. The geopolitical culture of an Internet company like Facebook is defined by its image of itself and the role it believes it is playing (or believes it should be playing). Is it a neutral platform promoting social networking or a mechanism for monetising data? Is it an innocent victim of cyber

25 Klaus Dodds: *Geopolitics: A Very Short Introduction*, Oxford University Press, 2014.
26 Toal: *Near Abroad*.
27 Toal: *Near Abroad*.
28 Toal: *Near Abroad*.

misbehaviour by others, or an independent geopolitical actor in its own right? The decisions and actions of Facebook will depend on the answers to these questions. The importance of geopolitical culture in the geopolitical behaviour of Internet companies is illustrated by Google's decision not to participate in the Pentagon's cloud project, and the controversy over its decision to collaborate in developing a filtered search engine for China.

The concept of geopolitical condition[29] seeks to capture the impact on the behaviour of states of assemblages of technology. Critical geopolitics seeks to understand how such assemblages of different technologies (eg military, transportation, communication) change the way in which geopolitics is experienced and practised. In a sense this picks up on Mackinder's insight of the potential importance of railways and the telegraph in transforming the internal communications of the Heartland. But again Mackinder was overly deterministic, not understanding that these technologies could be understood or experienced in different ways, which would affect the way they would be used. Critical geopolitics also argues that technological systems have a life of their own and create ecologies that influence how states operate within geopolitical fields and their geopolitical cultures. The importance of technology assemblages in Cyberspace is clear. Cyberspace itself has become a virtual ecology which influences the behaviour of state and non-state actors. Increasingly analysts talk of a digital ecosystem in which state and non-state actors operate and interact, in ways structured by the Internet.[30] But not all actors experience or understand Cyberspace in the same way. For some actors it represents liberation, for others a commercial opportunity, for others a threat and for some all of the above. How actors, state or non-state, experience and understand Cyberspace will affect their behaviour.

The concept of technological assemblages conditioning how actors behave geopolitical fields and develop their geopolitical culture reminds us that we should not see Cyberspace only in the sense of digital technologies. Firstly, of course, Cyberspace and the Internet are supported by multiple digital technologies. It is the way that these technologies have come together in an assemblage that has created Cyberspace in the first place. Thus Cyberspace itself is a multi-technology assemblage. But digital technologies are also combining with other new disruptive technologies, for example drones, AI, machine learning, or quantum computing, which will transform how Cyberspace operates (eg the implications of quantum computing for encryption and what this could

29 Toal: *Near Abroad*.

30 Jorge Perez Martinez and Zoraida Frias Barroso: *A Level Playing Field for the Digital Ecosystem*, Telefónica, 2016.

mean for surveillance). But not all actors will experience these technologies in the same way. The way in which they experience and understand them will depend on their geopolitical culture, and in turn influence the future evolution of that culture. That in turn will influence how they behave, what uses they will make of these new technological assemblages, in different geopolitical fields.

Dittmer[31] expands this concept into diplomatic assemblages. These include states, their foreign policy apparatuses and the buildings and people that compose them. Dittmer argues that national interest is not dictated by geography or by economic necessity but materialises through a series of assemblages including think tanks, political parties, universities, embassies, lobbying groups and media networks. These interact with each other and coalesce for a time around a series of policy documents. These assemblages are dynamic over time, meaning that in certain times and places some elements will matter more, but that in others this will change. Dittmer places particular emphasis in his analysis of diplomatic assemblages on the importance of things, whether buildings or archives, as well as technologies in influencing policy decisions. One of his case studies is the development of the British Foreign Office in the 19th century, in which he shows how the production and reception of paper (in the form of diplomatic documents) overwhelmed the ability of the existing foreign office to cope. This combined with the weaknesses of the existing building led to the design of the new building, but also shaped the context in which British foreign policy was made. The author's own experiences of the way in which paper flows and the physical structure of the Foreign and Commonwealth Office, as well as its Whitehall location in relation to other Government ministries, tend to confirm Dittmer's analysis and intuitions.

Cyberspace does not eradicate the impact of things and spaces on foreign policy decision-making, but it does alter the way in which they work. Building on Dittmer's example of the paper flow can make the point. In the 1950s and 60s policy documents in the British Foreign Office were typed by secretaries from hand written drafts prepared by Foreign Office officials. The policy documents would be agreed at department level before being submitted through a hierarchical process to more senior officials, culminating, if the issue were serious enough, in the Foreign Secretary. Copies were made by the use of carbon paper. This meant that unless multiple copies were to be typed, the number of copies that could be made of a document was limited to three. This meant both that careful thought had to be given about to whom to copy the documents, and also that the consultation process prior to submitting the policy recommendations tended to be limited. This had both advantages and disadvantages:

31 Dittmer: *Diplomatic Material*.

individual policy recommendations would be considered by only a narrow group of officials and experts, but the process was quicker and more flexible. This was changed by the introduction of photocopiers in the 1970s. Officials could now copy policy documents to as many officials and departments, both inside and outside the Foreign Office as they liked, or as the department paper allocation allowed. Distribution lists for documents grew. This allowed much wider consultation on policy recommendations, but also slowed down the process. Copy addressees of draft policy recommendations were under pressure to comment to ensure they, or their department, would be copied into future documents. Agreeing policy recommendations became a complicated process of multi-departmental discussions, which not only made the whole process more cumbersome, but also tended to lead to bland policy recommendations representing the lowest common denominator. Digital technologies, which were adopted relatively late in the Foreign Office because of lingering security concerns, have further encouraged this process. Additional copies of documents, sent electronically, are now resource free, encouraging officials to copy policy recommendations even more widely, including to embassies abroad. In the case of non-security sensitive recommendations, they can even be copied to non-state actors with whom the Foreign Office is collaborating. Digital technologies make the transmission of draft policy recommendations virtually instantaneous (depending if the recipient has turned on his device) and offer alternative more flexible channels for exchanging recommendations and comments (eg encrypted messenger services like WhatsApp). But they also allow, and even encourage, more iterations of comments and responses. Ironically, digital technologies may be less resource intensive and more efficient in copying policy recommendations throughout the policy-making network, but less efficient in the actual policy making process. This illustrates how new technologies have not removed the impact of "things", like paper flows, on policy-making, but simply changed the ways we have to think about them. The 21st century Foreign Office may not sink under the weight of paperwork, as the 19th century Downing Street Foreign Office described by Dittmer literally did, but it may drown in in comments and debate on policy-making.

Dittmer's concept of diplomatic assemblage allows us to explore the way in which people, institutions and physical and virtual objects interact to influence how key state and non-state actors behave in Cyberspace. It combines usefully with the concepts of geopolitical culture and geopolitical conditions. If one of the key foci of geopolitical conditions for the purposes of this article is how different actors experience and understand Cyberspace in different ways, and what that means for their geopolitical culture and behaviour in different geopolitical fields, the concept of diplomatic assemblage helps understand why different actors have those different experiences. As Dittmer comments,[32] assemblage analysis highlights the importance of the heterogenous and micro. While grand strategic or doctrinal narratives can be developed to explain the behaviour of major players in Cyberspace, that behaviour also depends on an interlocking network of institutions, individuals, technologies, structures and events. Cyberspace does, however, demand one amendment to the concept of diplomatic assemblages. In Dittmer's conception, non-state actors feature as possible components in a diplomatic assemblage. The assemblage is owned by the state, which makes the foreign policy decisions. In Cyberspace we have to accept that non-state actors, in as far as they are seen as independent geopolitical actors, by themselves or others, possess their own diplomatic assemblages which influence their decisions and actions. As with the assemblages of states, the components in the assemblages of non-state actors vary in importance over time, modifying the attitudes and actions of the non-state actors.

5 Cyberspace

There are no formally agreed definitions of Cyberspace, which is often seen as coterminous with the Internet. However, this article will argue that the two are not the same. Cyberspace extends beyond the Internet to encompass the state and non-state actors that use it, while the Internet provides the "geographical" structure underlying it. According to the 2009 British Government definition:[33] "Cyberspace includes all forms of networked, digital activities; this includes the content of and actions conducted through digital networks." An alternative approach[34] is to think of Cyberspace consisting of four layers: physical, logic, data and social. The first three layers constitute what we call the Internet, and condition the ways in which different state and non-state actors experience and understand Cyberspace, shaping geopolitical cultures and the ways these actors behave in geopolitical fields. Kello[35] has argues that we should distinguish between Cyberspace (consisting of the Internet including the World Wide Web and the cyber archipelagos) and cyberdomain, which covers human interactions in Cyberspace. But this seems an unnecessary distinction. Moreover, by distinguishing between technical and human domains,

32 Dittmer: *Diplomatic Material.*

33 The UK Cybersecurity Strategy: https://assets.publishing.service.gov.uk/Government/uploads/system/uploads/attachment_data/file/228841/7642.pdf.

34 Klimburg: *The Darkening Web.*

35 Lucas Kello: *The Virtual Weapon and International Order*, Yale, 2017.

it can imply that the lower levels of the former are not political. Indeed some commentators do distinguish between political and technical problems in Cyberspace. But, as is becoming clear, all levels in Cyberspace are highly political, and geopolitical, and politicised.

Some commentators have argued that Cyberspace is flat and without structures. As a virtual world it is without borders, and is able to transgress the national borders in the physical world. Khanna[36] argues that this cross-border interconnectivity will undermine the traditional nation state, replacing it with regionally integrated coastal megacities. Others argue that direct contact between civil societies will bypass Governments, rendering them irrelevant.[37] It is undoubtedly true that the development of the Internet has empowered a broad range of non-state actors, facilitating their participation in international debates, for example over climate change or human rights. Such non-state actors include not only the familiar NGOs like Greenpeace and Amnesty International, but also companies, city and regional Governments (as Khanna identifies) and a whole host of smaller and less formal groups who are able to gather information in ways previously reserved for Governments and network at an international level. An interesting example is Bellingcat. Bellingcat[38] is a website founded by British citizen journalists which scours publicly available images and videos to uncover misbehaviour by state actors. Its successes include identifying the use of barrel bombs and cluster munitions in Syria, the Russian missile launcher which brought down MH17 over the Ukraine and the identities of those suspected of poisoning the Skripals in the UK. This would have been inconceivable only a few years ago. Non-state actors on "the dark side", range from Islamic terrorists to organised criminal gangs. There are also the major Internet companies, although, as this article will argue later, these fall into a separate category.

While the Internet has facilitated the participation in international relations of this broad range of non-state actors, Khanna's declaration of the death of the nation state may be premature. In recent years the importance of the nation state in physical space has been strengthened by the re-appearance of more traditional international agendas centred on competition for territory, influence and resources. Thus Russia has effectively seized territory in Georgia as well as Ukraine, while China projects sovereignty claims into the South China Sea. The resurgence in the role of the nation state when security concerns are prevalent was already seen following the 9/11 and other Islamic terrorist

36 Parag Khanna: *Connectography: Mapping the Global Network Revolution*, W&N, 2017.

37 Jean-Marie Guehenno: *The End of the Nation State*, University of Minnesota Press, 2000.

38 https://www.bellingcat.com.

attacks, which have allowed an unprecedented level of Government surveillance in western societies. A similar logic appears to function in Cyberspace. As concerns grow about the different aspects of cybersecurity (which this article will exam later), the role of Governments increases. In part this is because, as in physical space, only Governments have both the capacity and the legitimacy to undertake the full range of security measures required, including offensive operations.

6 The Geography of Cyberspace

The way in which the Internet functions as "geography" can be seen by examining how each of the Internet layers of Cyberspace interact with key state actors. The lowest, physical level, consists of the hardware on which the Internet depends: the fibre optic cables on which data is carried, the Internet exchange points (IXPs) and the data centres of the Internet Service Providers (ISPs). Because of the way the Internet developed originally as Arpanet, part of US military research, the overwhelming majority of hardware remains within the US. The US has by far the largest number of IXPs (83). Because of the network package switching which underlies the operation of the Internet, and the prevalence of ISP data centres, some 80% of Internet traffic passes through fibre optic cables in US territory.[39] This generates some physical vulnerabilities. A crucial underwater fibre optic cable runs from the west coast of the UK to the US, carrying a significant percentage of global Internet traffic. British military officials are concerned about the interest Russian submarines have been showing in this cable, and have dispatched British submarines to monitor their activities. It is not clear whether the Russian submarines are preparing to place taps on or cut the cables. The latter would have a dramatic effect on the operating of the global Internet. Ironically, the British know all about the importance of cutting cables: the first hostile act the UK took in the World War I was to cut the German transatlantic telegraph cable, forcing the Germans to use British cables (and allowing the British to read German diplomatic cables).[40]

But this prevalence of physical infrastructure in the US, and the sheer quantity of Internet traffic which passes over US controlled fibre optic cables, also shapes the ways in which other actors experience Cyberspace. This was

39 Klimburg: *The Darkening Web*.
40 Gordon Corera: *Intercept: The Secret History of Computers and Spies*, Orion Books, 2015.

made clear when Edward Snowden[41] revealed the extent to which the National Security Agency (NSA) was tapping into the Internet as part of surveillance operations. This did not necessarily mean that the NSA was reading individual emails, although it was doing that too. Without going that far, it was able to analyse the meta data, the patterns of data flows in the Internet (a technique first developed during the Second World War). The 80% of Internet data passing through the US gave it a singular advantage. Other actors began to experience Cyberspace as being drawn into US surveillance operations. Even as they had to continue to use the Internet, they grew concerned about the security of their data, whether of individuals or Governments. In Europe this led to proposals of a Schengen only Internet network, where data would circulate on cables physically within the Schengen zone (the borderless security zone within the European Union). China, on the other, hand is increasingly including fibre optic cables and other Internet infrastructure projects within its Belt Road Initiative (BRI) to re-balance the perceived US domination. This is sometimes referred to as the Digital Silk Road.

Hovering between the physical and logical levels of the Internet are its network structure (and that of the World Wide Web – the global network of web-pages that allow most users to access the Internet). A popular theory holds that the Internet was designed to ensure the survival of US military command and control in the event of a nuclear attack. That is only partially true. Paul Baran[42] at the Rand Organisation was asked to explore this in the early 1960s, but his proposal of (effectively) packet switching on a distributive network (with massive inbuilt redundancy) was rejected by AT&T, who then enjoyed a monopoly over US telecommunications. The packet switching was resurrected when Arpa developed the Arpanet to, initially, link universities working on defence projects. The network itself was not designed but allowed to develop as Arpanet grew and later developed into the Internet. Studies by Barabási[43] and others have concluded that the Internet is not a distributed but scale free network. This means that while most nodes have very few links to other nodes, some nodes have very large numbers of links (in other words the relationship between nodes and links follows a power law distribution). This scale free network, or power law distribution, is repeated in the world wide web, where most webpages have relatively few links, but some have millions. This means that both the Internet and world wide web are more resilient than high-

41 Luke Harding: *The Snowden Files: The Inside Story of the World's Most Wanted Man*, Guardian Faber, 2014.

42 https://www.rand.org/about/history/baran.html.

43 Albert-Laszlo Barabasi: *Linked: The New Science of Networks*, Perseus, 2003.

ly centralised networks, but are constructed around a relatively small number of major hubs. Taking out a significant number of these hubs would not immediately take down the Internet, but the cascading effect as data had to be re-routed away from the hubs taken out would risk overwhelming other hubs eventually paralysing the flow of data. Thus the "geography" of the Internet would leave it vulnerable to a determined and targeted attack on key hubs.[44]

From a geopolitical point of view, the most interesting aspect of this scale free network of the Internet and world wide web is that these hubs are geographically situated in the physical world. Although the companies associated with these major hubs, the Googles, Amazons and Facebooks, to name but three, operate around the world, there headquarters are physically centred on the US, and primarily Silicon Valley. They see themselves as American companies, and are seen as such by their users and state and non-state actors. This again shapes the experience these actors have when engaging with Cyberspace, increasing fears among some of US hegemony. But there is another aspect that reflects developments in the physical world. The concentration of hubs is progressively moving east. This can be seen in the world wide web with the exponential growth of Chinese Internet company sites like Alibaba, WeChat or Weibo. As China grows as regional hegemon in the physical world, it does so also in Cyberspace. The geography of the Internet is changing.

7 Internet Governance

The data level of the Internet is the level at which the rules and protocols are agreed and operate to ensure that the data carried on the Internet gets to its destination. These rules and protocols and the way in which they are regulated grew out of how the Internet was developed by academics, engineers and computer entrepreneurs. Kello[45] points out that the development of the TCP/-IP protocols "prioritised the successful delivery" of packets of data "over accounting of the sender's identity and their content". At the time in which Internet protocols were being designed this made sense. But it built a significant insecurity into the heart of the Internet's structure, and a significant advantage for attack over defence in cybersecurity. It is too late to change it now. The geography of the Internet matters.

International institutions tend to reflect the geopolitical power balance of the moment of their creation, and be designed for the concerns of that time.

44 Philip Ball: *Critical Mass: How One Thing Leads to Another*, Arrow, 2005.

45 Kello: *The Virtual Weapon and International Order*.

As the balance of power and concerns change, the institution ceases to be fit for purpose. Thus the UN Security Council was designed to deal with interstate conflict, with a permanent membership reflecting the major powers in 1945 (no-one would seriously propose the UK and France as permanent members in 2019). In many respects the Internet is an international institution, and its governance structures reflect the moment and place of its birth. It was born at the moment of US hegemony, sometimes called the unipolar moment.[46] This ensured a single global Internet. Had the Internet emerged a decade earlier, during the Cold War, it would undoubtedly not have been universal. There would have been a Soviet Internet, a NATO Internet, a Chinese Internet and perhaps a non-aligned Internet. If the Internet had emerged now, once the unipolar moment had passed, there would probably be US, China, Russian and EU Internets, all mutually incompatible in some respect. A recent New York Times editorial[47] has even suggested the Internet could split into two or three parts in ten to fifteen years. The recent arguments about the involvement of the Chinese telecommunications company Huawei in setting industry standards for 5G mobile telephony threaten the prospect of separate, only partially compatible, 5G systems developing at international level[48]

The place of the Internet's birth also shaped its regulatory framework. Silicon Valley in the 90s still reflected a hippy-like distrust of authority and Government, and a certain entrepreneurial independence. This combination of moment and place of creation has left the Internet with a unique governance structure, largely non-Governmental and driven by engineers and technicians. For example, the allocation of domain names and numbers is governed by ICANN[49] (the Internet Corporation for Assigned Names and Numbers), a not-for-profit company registered in the State of California. ICANN was originally contracted by the US Commerce Department to carry out the IANA (Internet Assigned Numbers Authority) on its behalf, but this role was transferred to ICANN in its own right. ICANN's governing body consists of nominated engineers, technicians and representatives of Internet companies. Government representatives are relegated to a Government advisory body. Some Governments, led by China, argue that a governance structure that was fit for purpose for networked university computers in the 1990s is no longer fit

46 Hal Brands: *Making the Unipolar Moment: US Foreign Policy and the Rise of the Post-Cold War Order*, Cornell, 2016.

47 https://www.nytimes.com/2018/10/15/opinion/Internet-google-china-balkanization.html.

48 http://thecorner.eu/world-economy/5g-the-real-reason-behind-us-attacks-on-huawei/78010/.

49 https://www.icann.org/es.

for purpose for a global public good in the 21st century and want Internet governance brought within an intergovernmental international organisation, possibly the existing International Telecommunications Union. Other countries, led by the US and the EU, want to maintain the multistakeholder nature of ICANN. So far the multistakeholder approach has been able to resist the pressures from the "multilateralists", but something akin to a new Cold War is developing over Internet governance between the Free Internet Nations and the Cyber Sovereignty Advocates.[50]

Splits are emerging among the Free Internet Nations, reflecting evolving geopolitical cultures, especially with the election of President Trump in the US and the progressive withdrawal of the US from providing global public goods as part of an international liberal order. A central objective of the Free Internet Nations has been to maintain net neutrality, the principle that all data being transmitted on the Internet is treated equally. Internet service providers have increasingly complained that this allows Internet media companies like YouTube or Netflix to make unfair profits while taking up an ever greater proportion of the bandwidth. They want to be able to treat different users in different ways in transmitting their data, possibly charging companies like YouTube or Netflix a higher commercial rate. While this seems reasonable, Free Internet Nations and their supporters have argued that this would open up the path to privileged Internet access for wealthier Internet users, increasing the existing digital divide, and even allow some users (eg dissidents) to be excluded altogether. However, in June 2018 the US Federal Communications Commission[51] voted to repeal the net neutrality provisions adopted by the Obama administration. It is yet to be seen what the international implications of this will be. The decision is being challenged in the courts, and several states, for example California, are insisting they will maintain net neutrality (although the Trump administration is in turn taking them to the Supreme Court for exceeding their constitutional powers). But the idea that something as fundamental as net neutrality could be decided unilaterally by the US Government on fundamentally commercial grounds will strengthen the arguments of the Cyber Sovereignty Advocates that the Internet is too important to be left to the multi-stakeholder model of governance, and should be brought within the purview of an international organisation.

---

50 Klimburg: *The Darkening Web.*

51 https://www.washingtonpost.com/gdpr-consent/?destination=%2fnews%2fthe-switch%2fwp%2f2017%2f12%2f14%2fthe-fcc-is-expected-to-repeal-its-net-neutrality-rules-today-in-a-sweeping-act-of-deregulation%2f%3f&utm_term=.ee86924da97e.

8 Cybersecurity

If the structures of the different levels of the Internet function as the geography of Cyberspace, generating an Internet governance agenda, then the actions that state and non-state actors take against other state and non-state actors constitute the cybersecurity agenda. It is important to stress here the word "against". State and non-state actors can take many actions in Cyberspace to influence each other that may be regarded as legitimate, for example using social media platforms as part of public diplomacy campaigns. The cybersecurity agenda deals with actions that at least one of the parties regards as illegitimate. There is indeed some ambiguity here. Legitimacy to some extent lies in the eye of the beholder, and until universally accepted definitions of unacceptable behaviour in Cyberspace have been established, is likely to remain there. Some activities clearly fall within the cybersecurity agenda, for example penetrating foreign computer systems to damage those systems, causing physical (kinetic) damage in the real world or stealing intellectual property or sensitive data. But other areas are more ambiguous. The difference between acceptable public diplomacy and information warfare is particularly fraught. As we will see, what we regard as Russian information warfare is seen by Russians as a response to our information warfare against them, which we in turn regard as acceptable public diplomacy.

The problems are compounded by the tendency of the public, and an overly excitable media, to lump together a variety of different activities under the moniker cyber attacks. This is dangerous. The use of the phrase "cyber attack" is itself misleading. Attacks in the physical world are aggressive actions that require a response, often in kind. We would not normally refer to an espionage attack. Espionage is a more or less continuous activity in which states seek to learn sensitive information about each other. States may not like being spied on by other states, but accept it on the basis that they are doing likewise. The same appears to be happening in Cyberspace. This may explain the muted response to the Snowden revelations by many non-European countries. Countries like China and Russia assume the US is carrying out cyberespionage against them: they are doing it to the US (European outrage arose not at the revelation of US cyberespionage operations, from which they too would often benefit, but rather that the Americans were spying on their friends as well as their rivals and enemies). Referring to cyberespionage "attacks" suggests that each one must be responded to. Given the current levels of cyberespionage activities, by all sides, this is unrealistic, and risks being escalatory. As we shall see, cyberespionage may also be a crucial part of cyber defence. The article also seeks to avoid the use of the term "cyberwar" (although to some extent it is stuck with it). Like cyber attack, cyberwar is used to cover a multitude of sins without clarifying exactly what is meant. If we associate warfare with physical damage to persons and infrastructure, then there may only have been one cyberwar operation. If we use it to refer more widely to attacks that seek to steal data, damage information systems or plant propaganda, then we may be forced to conclude that we are already in a war in Cyberspace, and not a cold one. This is not necessarily a conclusion we would want to reach, or one that we would reach if we were more nuanced in our use of language.[52]

For the purposes of this article, the cybersecurity agenda refers to activities undertaken by states, or their non-state surrogates, against other states for political or geopolitical reasons. These activities amount to penetrations of foreign computer systems or the use of online platforms for pursuing information warfare. It does not refer to activities undertaken for criminal reasons, whether by state or non-state actors. This latter activity does fall within cybersecurity but not within geopolitics. The distinction may be questionable, and the intersection between political and criminal activities in Cyberspace and its implications for diplomacy and foreign policy is certainly worthy of further investigation. The major Internet companies, which this article argues are a separate case, is looked at later.

Valeriano et al[53] distinguish between three objectives for the penetration of the computer systems of foreign states: degeneration; disruption; and espionage. Degeneration refers to causing long term or permanent damage to information systems, possibly with impact in the physical world (kinetic damage). Disruption refers to short term disruption of computer systems, which could have Kinetic effect. For example, the ransomware "Wannacry" attack, although criminal rather than political, blocked computers at some hospitals in the UK and led to the postponement of operations and other medical treatment. Espionage looks to steal data to acquire information about intentions and capabilities, intellectual property that can be used to commercial or military advantage, or materials that can be used in subsequent information operations. Libicki[54] offers a slightly different triology: advanced persistent attack (APT), Distributed Denial of Services Attack (DDOS) and destructive attack. The problem with this trilogy, apart from its insistence in the use of the word "attack", is that it confuses method with outcome in its typology. Thus DDOS describes a method of disruption, whereby a computer virus is used to oblige

52 http://www.shaunriordan.com/?p=636.

53 Brandon Valeriano, Benjamin Jensen and Ryan C Maness: *Cyber Strategy: The Evolving Character of Power and Coercion*, Oxford University Press, 2018.

54 Martin C Libicki: *Cyberspace in Peace and War*, Naval Institute Press, 2016.

large numbers of computers to send simultaneous requests for information to a website, overwhelming its ability to respond (in this case, it is not the target which is penetrated, but the computers unwittingly co-opted for the attack). Likewise, APT describes a long term penetration of foreign computer systems, whether to gather information or prepare for future degenerative action. However, "destructive" describes the outcome, however it is achieved. Nye[55] in turn distinguishes between Computer Network Exploitation (ex-filtration of confidential information against the wishes of the owner) and Computer Network Attack (using information to disrupt and destroy). But this does not really distinguish between operations aimed at permanent (including kinetic) damage and operations aimed only at short term disruption. In terms of policy responses, this is a significant distinction. This article will essentially use Valeriano's typology, but add a further category of information operations, where states seek to use Cyberspace to undermine or destabilise foreign Governments and societies.

Valeriano et al[56] argue that states seeking to maintain power prefer degeneration operations; states rising in power prefer espionage operations; and states falling in power prefer disruption operations. They do not mean that each different kind of state exclusively uses that kind of operation, but this does seem overly determinist, much like geographic determinism in classical geopolitics. The kind of cyberoperations states or their non-state surrogates, undertake will also depend on geopolitical cultures, the geopolitical fields in which they are operating and the effect of geopolitical conditions.[57] For example, a state might not see itself as falling in power, even if others do, and its preference for disruption operations might arise from the way it has experienced Cyberspace (including its perception of how others might operate in Cyberspace) and the influence of pre-existing military doctrines. There may also be diplomatic assemblage effects.[58] The cyber operational decisions of a state seeking to maintain its power may be affected by a combination of national self-image, the interaction between different Government agencies, the domestic political environment the personal relationships between key political figures and relations with other countries, including allies, and the technology available.

---

55 Joseph Nye: *Deterrence and Dissuasion in Cyberspace*, International Security, vol 41, no 3 (Winter 2016/17: https://www.belfercenter.org/sites/default/files/files/publication/isec_a_00266.pdf).

56 Valeriano et al: *Cyber Strategy*.

57 Toal: *Near Abroad*.

58 Dittmer: *Diplomatic Material*.

Valeriano et al[59] also, wisely (see above), recommend talking about cyber coercion rather than cyberwar. From the case studies they have done, they conclude that only degeneration operations seem to have compellence effect, compelling a rival to do something he did not want to. Although the only clear cut degeneration operation so far is the so-called Stuxnet attack against the Iranian nuclear programme, and it remains uncertain to what extent this really compelled Iran to change its behaviour, or led to its participation in the 2015 Joint Comprehensive Plan of Action (JCPOA – the article will look at this in more detail in the context of the US as a geopolitical actor in Cyberspace). The implication may be that the level of cyber operations that have occurred so far have had a greater psychological than physical effect, generating uncertainty rather compelling behaviour. This is not to say that degeneration attacks cannot be conceived of that could have compellence effects, for example attacks with severe Kinetic effects on critical infrastructure, but as Valeriano et al point out, for whatever reason, there have been no such attacks so far. Indeed, the vast majority of cyber operations so far have been disruption or espionage attacks. Valeriano et al characterise disruption attacks as essentially the weaponization of information. They point out that even such disruption attacks can have significant Kinetic effects. The UAE sponsored penetration of computers in the official Qatar news agency in 2017, and the posting of a fake statement by the Emir of Qatar praising Iran and Hamas, criticising Trump and talking of good relations with Israel, served as a catalyst for the blockade of Qatar by Saudi Arabia and its Gulf allies.[60]

But by their characterisation of disruption as the weaponization of information, they overlook the use of disruption operations as low cost and low risk weapons of punishment. The massive DDOS operations against Estonia's computer systems in 2007, whether carried out by the Russian Government or (as Russia claims) by outraged Russian patriots, aimed to punish Estonia for removing a statue commemorating Soviet war dead in the Second World War. It is arguable that apparently Russian inspired attacks on Ukraine's power grid in 2015 and 2016[61] were also disruption operations: their effects were short-lived and caused more inconvenience than real damage (they may also have been a form of signalling, to both Kiev and Washington). Neither of these disruption operations really amounts to the weaponization of information. And by focusing on disruption operations, Valeriano et al may have missed the

59 Valeriano et al: *Cyber Strategy*.

60 https://www.nytimes.com/2017/06/08/world/middleeast/qatar-cyberattack-espionage-for-hire.html?_r=0.

61 David Sanger: *The Perfect Weapon: Sabotage and Fear in the Cyber Age*, Scribe UK, 2018.

real weaponization of information: the use of social media and other online platforms to spread dis and misinformation aimed at destabilising foreign societies and undermining and fragmenting political and social discourse, what US diplomat George Kennan would have called "Political Warfare" and the Soviets "Active Measures". The article will consider the extent to which Russia has been using such information operations, especially during the 2016 Brexit referendum and US Presidential elections in the context of Russia as a geopolitical actor in Cyberspace.

9 International Law in Cyberspace

Conflict, including armed conflict, in physical space is constrained by a series of rules and norms that have been codified over the years: the UN Charter, The Laws of Armed Conflict (LOAC) and international humanitarian law, as well as a series of multilateral treaties and conventions on specific aspects of conflict (eg Geneva Convention on prisoners of war or the ban on land mines). Such laws do not act as domestic law. Outside the UN Security Council, which seems to have returned to the blockage of the Cold War, there is little effective international sanction against states. The extent to which states, or their leaders, can be sanctioned tends to be conditioned by their size and importance in the international system. To give the full quotation from the Melian Dialogue: "Justice exists only between equals. Otherwise the strong do what they will and the weak what they can."[62] But in a sense this is not how international law functions. Generally states do not decide their foreign policy in accordance with the dictates of international law. Rather they decide their foreign policy in accordance with their perception of their interests, and then adapt it to appear as if it falls within international law.[63] They do so partly to be seen to remain within the international community of states,[64] and partly to fit with their self-image (albeit self-delusional) as a law-abiding and responsible state. This may appear cynical, and yet it does act as a constraint on the behaviour of even the most aggressive states, provided that they see themselves as members of the international community of states and wish to remain so. Russian behaviour in the Ukraine in 2014 makes the point.[65] Russia seized the Crimea, but made sure it did so with troops not wearing insignia. Russia's official

62 Thucydides: *The History of the Peloponnesian War*, Penguin, 2000.
63 Shaun Riordan: *Cyberdiplomacy: Managing Security and Governance Online*, Polity, 2019.
64 Barry Buzan: *An Introduction to the English School of International Relations*, Polity, 2014.
65 Toal: *Near Abroad*.

presence was deferred until it had staged a referendum on Crimea's wish to become part of Russia. Although this was transparently fraudulent in Western eyes, it allowed Putin to claim a comparison with the self-determination of Kosovo by force of western arms (in Putin's eyes at least). Although Russia destabilised Eastern Ukraine, it did not attempt to seize Ukraine (as militarily it could have) as there was no semi-legal justification it could construct for this, and it would clearly have placed Russian outside the international community and its norms.[66]

It is not clear how international law and the various rules and norms of armed conflict apply to Cyberspace, if indeed they do. The UN established Group of Government Experts (GGE) appeared to agree at one point that all international law applied in Cyberspace, but both the Russians and the Chinese have subsequently rowed back from that agreement.[67] The GGE did reach some early agreements, for example on not attacking Computer Emergency Rescue Teams (CERTs), but the process seems to have stalled and it is not clear if it will continue. The European Council's Convention on Cybercrime (the Budapest Convention) seeks to prohibit some activities in Cyberspace, including data and information theft, but China and Russia are among the major countries who have not signed it.[68] Within NATO, the Tallinn Manual[69] (an initiative launched after the 2007 DDOS attacks on Estonia) seeks to establish principles for dealing with conflict in Cyberspace. Among other features, it distinguishes between cyberattacks that do not amount to a use of force; cyberattacks that do amount to a use of force but not an armed attack and cyber attacks which amount to an armed attack. But these principles apply only within NATO, and amount more to guidelines for responding to cyber operations than rules of behaviour. A group of cybersecurity experts meeting in Las Vegas adopted the Las Vegas rules of behaviour in Cyberspace.[70] These include the principle that any attack in Cyberspace should also be responded to with an attack in Cyberspace, and not in physical space. But these are only suggestions and not binding.

66 Total: *Near Abroad.*

67 Klimburg: *The Darkening Web.*

68 Adam Segal: *The Hacked World Order: How Nations Fight, Trade, Maneuver and Manipulate in the Digital Age*, Public Affairs, 2017.

69 Libicki: *Cyberspace in Peace and War.*

70 Libicki: *Cyberspace in Peace and War.*

10 Attribution

There are features of Cyberspace that mean that principles of international law and behaviour in physical space cannot simply be transferred. This is illustrated by the problem of attribution. In inter-state conflict in physical space it is usually clear who an attacker is, ie which state has launched an aggressive attack against another. The US knew who had attacked it on Pearl Harbour. Article 51 of the UN Charter which enshrines the right of self-defence against aggression assumes the straightforward identification of the aggressor. Attribution can be more complicated with attacks by non-state actors, for example terrorist attacks. However, even then terrorist attacks are usually attributed quite quickly and with considerable accuracy. Indeed, most terrorist groups are only too happy to take the credit for their attacks. The problem is more likely to be deciding between multiple claimants. Governments do sometimes get attribution of terrorist attacks wrong, for example when the Spanish Government initially attributed the Atocha train bombings in 2004 to the Basque terrorist group ETA rather than an Islamist group, but these errors are usually quickly corrected. The US authorities were swiftly and accurately able to identify Al Qaeda's responsibility for the 9/11 attacks.

Attribution in Cyberspace is much harder. Hackers, whether state or non-state, often seek to conceal their identity. They have a range of techniques to use to achieve this, ranging from virtual private networks (VPNs), operating through or from third countries or using viruses to hijack other parties' computers. Governments make seek to distance themselves by working through non-state proxies, whether "patriotic" or criminal hackers. Cybersecurity experts have a range of techniques at their disposal to attribute cyber penetrations, and claim that they are improving in both speed and accuracy. This has been shown by the ability of the US to attribute attacks not only to specific countries, but also specific intelligence officers, who have then been indicted, in both China and Russia. However, attribution remains difficult and time consuming. Initial attributions may prove inaccurate and need to be corrected later. The Ransomware attack Wannacry, although criminal rather than political, was initially attributed to Russian hackers. Only later was it concluded that N Korean hackers were the most likely culprits. In the case of a serious cyberattack with Kinetic effects a Government needs the capability to respond quickly, both to reassure its citizens and to deter further attacks. Identifying the source of the attack over a six month period with a degree of certainty of 70% is not good enough. An additional complication is false flag operations, in which the hacker deliberately makes the hack look as if it has come from another country. This creates the danger of retaliation against a third innocent country, provoking a separate cyberconflict with that country. Technical solutions may further improve the speed and confidence of attribution, but it is going to remain a serious problem in responding to cyber operations.

11 The Cybersecurity Dilemma

Buchanan[71] has explored how the classical security dilemma functions in Cyberspace and has concluded that it becomes more difficult to manage. In the classical security dilemma, country A fears the military superiority of country B. It embarks on a programme of arms purchases and other measures to improve its security situation. Country B interprets these moves as hostile, and embarks on own its programme of arms purchases and security enhancements. Country A ends up worse off than it was in the first place. The classic example is the Anglo-German arms race before World War I. In the Cyberspace version of the security dilemma, country A is concerned that country B is about to penetrate its computer systems in a degeneration attack. Country A looks to enhance its security by penetrating the computer systems of country B to better understand its intentions and capabilities. Country B interprets Country A's move as a hostile preparation for future degeneration attacks, and responds by increasing its penetration of country B's computer systems. Again Country A ends up worse off.

The problem in the classical security dilemma is that country B interprets country A's moves to improve its security as hostile moves against country B, rather than defensive measures. There is a misinterpretation of what is going on. The cybersecurity dilemma is worse, in the sense that there is no way of distinguishing between a defensive penetration to ascertain capabilities and intentions, and an offensive penetration aimed at preparing for a future degeneration operation, with or without kinetic affects. The US, for example, is aware that Russia has penetrated the computer systems operating its civilian critical infrastructure, but does not know if these are essentially surveillance or espionage operations, preparations for future destructive attacks with Kinetic effects, or signalling of what the Russians can do (referred to as pwnage in the hacking world).[72] The nature of Cyberspace also reduces or abolishes the various options for mitigating the security dilemma in physical space. In physical

71 Ben Buchanan: *The Cybersecurity Dilemma: Network Intrusions, Trust and Fear in the International System*, C Hurst & Co, 2017.

72 https://www.theguardian.com/us-news/2018/mar/15/russia-sanctions-energy-sector-cyber-attack-us-election-interference.

space it is possible to distinguish between offensive and defensive weapons (eg fighter aircraft are essentially defensive whereas bomber aircraft are clearly offensive). The type of weapons that country A is acquiring can help signal to country B whether its intentions are defensive or offensive. Likewise, the geographical location of new weapons systems, close to borders or in more reserved situations can also signal offensive or defensive intentions. Neither of these mitigating factors apply in Cyberspace.

12 Deterrence

The lack of visibility, and differentiation, in cyber weapons also causes problems with deterrence. Unlike in the Cold War, analysts cannot study pictures of missiles on flatback lorries being trundled through Red Square to assess the deterrence capability of an adversary (although a stream of flatback lorries each with a laptop on its back is an appealing thought). Even penetrating another country's computer systems to identify their cyber capabilities (as discussed above) may not be sufficient. As Libicki[73] points out, by penetrating another country's systems, a Government may identify some of the country's capabilities and intentions, but not all of them. Given the difficulty in differentiating between cyber tools until they are used (degeneration, disruption and espionage can all look pretty much alike), the scope for misunderstanding is considerable. But this also makes deterrence harder. In a sense, cyberweapons only exist when they are used, by when it is too late to deter. One state can threaten dire retaliation in return for a hostile cyber penetration, but the other state may doubt its commitment or whether it is truly capable of penetrating its systems or delivering on the threat. Revealing the scope of one's capabilities to penetrate another state's computer systems may put at risk one's ability to do so, as the state immediately strengthens its cybersecurity, focusing on the weaknesses one has revealed. If a state reveals that it has developed zero day exploits (previously unknown flaws in an operating system) which will allow it to penetrate a foreign computer system, rather than deter it will most likely provoke the computer company that designed the software to develop a patch to repair the flaw. If, on the other hand, a state announces that it has already penetrated a foreign computer system in preparation for cyber retaliation if and when needed, it risks revealing how it has penetrated the system, and putting a premature end to its penetration. This suggests that deterrence in

73 Libicki: *Cyberspace in Peace and War*.

Cyberspace may require threats of retaliation in physical space to be credible and effective (this will be discussed further below).

Nye[74] argues that this takes too narrow an approach to deterrence, based only on the threat of punishment, and that deterrence also includes denial by defence (making the cost of mounting an attack greater than the possible benefits), entanglement (growing interdependence in Cyberspace means that everyone, including the attacker, suffers the consequences of an attack) and normative taboos (whereby a potential attacker's self-image discourages him from carrying out an attack). The latter relates to a previous discussion of how international law functions,[75] and will be picked up again when we discuss the implications of the geopolitics of Cyberspace for diplomacy.

13 Arms Control

Another consequence of the difficulty in distinguishing between different types of cyber weapon maybe a re-ordering of the concept of arms limitation. In physical space arms limitation or disarmament talks have focused on specific types of weapons and sought to restrict their numbers or use, or on occasion prohibit their use altogether (eg landmines, or chemical or biological weapons). This approach makes little sense in Cyberspace. It would amount to prohibiting zero day exploits, but not spear phishing for example, or certain kinds of bots or viruses used to infect third party computers. Even if agreement could be reached on definitions of the different kinds of weapons, the attribution issue and the large scale presence of non-state actors would make it impossible to police. A more profitable approach may be to focus on the targets of cyberattacks, negotiating at international level certain categories of target against which attacks should not deliberately be launched. As Nye[76] puts it, the taboo may "not be against types of weapon systems, but against certain types of targets". There is already precedent in physical space with states prohibited from deliberately targeting civilians (as much honoured in the breach as in the observance). A similar approach in Cyberspace would focus on excluding civilian critical infrastructure (hospitals, emergency communications systems, air traffic control systems) from deliberate cyber attack. It would not be easy. There are definitional problems and dual usage issues (eg communications systems and air traffic control systems used both by civilians and the military).

74 Nye: *Deterrence and Dissuasion in Cyberspace.*
75 Shaun Riordan: *Cyberdiplomacy.*
76 Nye: *Deterrence and Dissuasion in Cyberspace.*

There will also be deliberate and accidental collateral damage in real cyber-conflict. But these are areas worth exploring.

14 Neutrality

A further difference between international law and norms in physical space and Cyberspace is the concept of neutrality.[77] In physical space, neutrality is a clearly defined concept in international law with both privileges and obligations. For example, the property of neutral states is subject to a degree of protection from the belligerents in a conflict. At the same time, a neutral state must prevent belligerent forces crossing its territory to attack another belligerent. Thus when Germany invaded Belgium in 1914, Belgium was confronted by the choice of resisting the German invasion, thus in effect becoming an ally of the UK and France, or allowing German passage through Belgium to attack France and in effect becoming a German ally. Either way it lost its neutrality (this will be relevant in subsequent discussion of the Internet companies as geopolitical actors). It is difficult to see how these ideas could be applied to Cyberspace. Given the complex cross-cutting and interdependence of the Internet, it would be difficult to identify in advance the property of neutral states, or to ensure that a degeneration operation to cause damage to the Internet equipment of a rival nation would not have collateral effects on the property of neutrals. Equally, it may be unreasonable to insist that in the case of conflict a neutral state should prevent a belligerent state passing through its territory to attack another. Given the packet switching operations of the Internet, a state would have no idea of the information passing through the fibre cables in its territory, or whether any of this data forms part of a hostile cyber attack causing disruption, degeneration or even kinetic damage in a third state. The concept of neutrality may need considerable re-working if it is to remain a viable concept in Cyberspace.

15 What Happens in Cyberspace Stays in Cyberspace …

A key issue will be whether a state must respond to a hostile cyber operation by a state or non-state actor only in Cyberspace, or whether retaliation can take place in physical space, including with Kinetic effect. The Las Vegas Rules,[78]

---

77 Libicki: *Cyberspace in Peace and War.*

78 Libicki: *Cyberspace in Peace and War.*

agreed by a meeting of computer and Internet technicians in Las Vegas, argue that what happens in Cyberspace should stay in Cyberspace. Responses and retaliation against cyberattacks should be carried out only in Cyberspace. Supporters of this view argue that it constrains the risks of escalation and encourages proportionate responses: there are limits to the damage that can be done through Cyberspace (certainly in comparison with the destruction that potentially can be wrought by kinetic attacks), and Governments understand that there are certain rules of the game.

However, the Tallinn Manual,[79] adopted by NATO following the massive cyber disruption operations against Estonia in 2007 allows for the possibility of responses to cyber operations in both physical and Cyberspace. In part this results from the difficulties of deterrence in Cyberspace discussed above. While threats of retaliation in Cyberspace may not be effective as a deterrent, in part because the lack of visibility of the threat, threats of retaliation in physical space may be more effective as deterrent because they are more visible and tangible. Thus in 2015, President Obama followed up the indictment of five Chinese military intelligence officers for cyberespionage by warning President Xi Jinping that the US would impose economic sanctions on China if it did not refrain from widespread online theft of US intellectual property. Obama and Xi subsequently signed an agreement not to steal intellectual property from each other. This may be an example of the threat of action in physical space acting as an effective deterrent in Cyberspace, although there may have been other reasons that President Xi wanted to reduce the levels of cyberespionage against the US (and other countries – he subsequently signed a similar agreement with the UK and the principles of the agreement were incorporated into the norms of the G20 in November 2015).[80]

Another reason for not wanting to restrict the response to cyber operations to Cyberspace is the problem of cyber vulnerability asymmetries (this is also relevant to Nye's[81] concept of deterrence through entanglement). A country's vulnerability to cyber operations depends on the extent of its integration into Cyberspace. The US is probably the most integrated country among the major powers, not only because of the Internet linkages between people, but also the increasing interconnections between devices, known as the Internet of Things (IoT). This integration and interdependence both increase the vulnerabilities to attack (attack vectors) and the possible impact of attacks. Societies less integrated offer fewer attack vectors and are likely to suffer less

79 Libicki: *Cyberspace in Peace and War.*
80 Adam Segal: *The Hacked World Order.*
81 Nye: *Deterrence and Dissuasion in Cyberspace.*

severe consequences from cyber operations. Thus if a cyberattack originating in North Korea (or more likely from North Korean agents operating abroad) causes significant degeneration or disruption in US Internet systems, it is difficult to see what kind of retaliatory cyber operation could achieve similar degeneration or disruption in North Korea. This is the cyber equivalent of the million dollar cruise missile destroying a ten dollar tent in Afghanistan. The same is true, to a lesser extent in Russia. Interestingly, although this once could have been said of China, China's rapid integration into Cyberspace is rendering it more vulnerable to cyber operations, which may be playing a role in a change of cyber strategy. Some western strategists argue that this asymmetric vulnerability requires the flexibility to respond to operations in Cyberspace with activities in physical space.[82]

In short Cyberspace has generated two types of international agenda: the Internet governance agenda and the cybersecurity agenda. They are inevitably interconnected, but there are differences between them, with the former engaging with a wider range of state and non-state actors and the former engaging mainly with states and their non-state surrogates. Despite the differences noted above, there are some parallels with the tensions between the New International Security Agenda (NISA), or Global Issues Agenda, and more traditional geopolitical agendas in physical space. They too are inter-related, but can distract attention from and undermine each other, with the more traditional geopolitical agendas demanding short term priority. There is the danger that the same could happen in Cyberspace, with the cybersecurity agenda being prioritised over, and undermining the attention paid to, the Internet governance agenda.

16 Geopolitics of States in Cyberspace

Having discussed the interaction between geopolitics and Cyberspace in general, the article now focuses on specific examples of states and regional Governments. It explores these examples to see if the concepts of classical and critical geopolitics, and diplomatic assemblages, can be applied to their activities in Cyberspace, and whether this yields interesting insights, either analytically or in terms of policy formulation. The article focuses on three states – the US, Russia and China – which have been prominent in Cyberspace, but which have adopted very different approaches. It also examines one regional grouping, the European Union (EU), which has taken a

82 Libicki: *Cyberspace in Peace and War*.

very distinctive path reflecting its broader approach to international relations. The article then explores a fifth group, the Internet companies like Facebook, Twitter, YouTube and Google. The key question with these companies is to what extent they should be recognised as geopolitical actors in Cyberspace in their own right (and to what extent they should self-recognise as geopolitical actors), and whether the kinds of geopolitical analysis examined in this article can be usefully applied to their activities.

17 The United States of America

17.1 *The US Experience of Cyberspace*

US hegemony in Cyberspace has been even greater than in physical space. When, following the end of the Cold War, the US achieved its unipolar moment,[83] it did so in a world inherited. The physical world the US dominated had evolved over hundreds of years of conflict, trade and debate. The rules governing international economic and political relations were as much European as they were American. The US could shape this world more in its own image, and tried to do so, but it was not starting with a blank sheet of paper. In contrast, Cyberspace was very much an American invention, originating originally in concerns about command and control under nuclear attack and then communications between defence scholars. Once escaped from the Defence Dept it evolved according to the needs and preferences of the technicians building it. It was a domain of activity very much designed in America's, or at least California's, image: entrepreneurial, non-hierarchical, libertarian and arm's length from Government and officialdom. Nothing symbolises this better than ICANN, the organisation tasked with allocating names and numbers in the Internet: a not for profit company, headquartered and registered in the state of California, originally contracted to the US Department of Commerce, where Government representatives are exiled to an advisory committee.[84]

Thus, for the first time in history, a hegemon was able to operate in a domain of its own creation. Cyberspace already reflected US values of libertarianism, freedom, free expression and free trade. Drawing on centuries of US exceptionalism, in the unilateral moment Cyberspace was, like the US itself, a force for good in the world. As Fukuyama announced the end of history and the triumph of US economic and political values, the US offered the Internet to the world as a domain in which these values could be promoted and realised.

83 Hal Brands: *Making the Unipolar Moment.*
84 Klimburg: *The Darkening Web.*

In terms of geopolitical conditions, the US experienced the Internet and Cyberspace as something it both created and owned. It gifted its creation to the rest of the world as an act of generosity from the global hegemon, and expected gratitude in return. It expected the world to accept the governance and operating rules of the Internet as part of the gift, and was surprised and resentful to the extent that these were challenged (reminiscent of the "why do they hate us?" debate after 9/11). Questioning the role of ICANN, or suggesting bringing Internet governance within intergovernmental bodies like the ITU were experienced as both lack of gratitude and hostile actions. The US experience of Cyberspace as their creation, to allow the rest of the world to benefit from engagement with US values, may also have meant that the US was slower to understand the dangers of Cyberspace, and its potential as a domain for interstate conflict. Both the Russians and, especially, the Chinese seem to have caught on to this earlier than Washington.[85]

If the geopolitical condition focuses on how the US experienced Cyberspace, geopolitical fields analyse the various levels in which the US operates in Cyberspace. At one level it is on its own, the global hegemon with unrivalled resources and capabilities for cyber operations, aiming, as its cyber strategy states, for "global network domination".[86] As we have discussed above, its high levels of Internet integration and dependency also leave it uniquely vulnerable to cyber operations, both in terms of available attack vectors and the impact of potential degeneration or disruption attacks. Like other liberal democracies, it is also more vulnerable to cyber information operations than more authoritarian regimes. But the US also operates at other levels, or in other geopolitics fields. In the debate over Internet governance it has traditionally been a leading figure in the Free Internet Nations, defending the multi-stakeholder model of Internet governance against the multinational model proposed by the Internet Sovereignty Advocates. Thus it has defended ICANN and, until recently, the e2e or net neutrality principle. This reflects its experience of the Internet as its creator and the one who gifted it to the world (as noted above).

17.2 *Geopolitical Fields of the US in Cyberspace*

The US also operates in multiple geopolitical fields in Cyberspace. As the largest member of NATO it has taken the lead in developing NATO's cybersecurity doctrine, including the Tallinn Manual, working closely with other NATO allies and particularly the Baltic Republics following the 2007 cyber disruption operation against Estonia and continual cyber operations in other Baltic Republics

85 Fred Kaplan: *Dark Territory: The Secret History of Cyber War*, Simon & Schuster, 2016.
86 Klimburg: *The Darkening Web*.

since. Cooperation with Ukraine, helping it deal with persistent Russian disruption operations, including against critical infrastructure like their power networks, is both an outreach from NATO and an effort to understand better Russian capabilities in the light of future possible operations against the US.[87] The US is the most powerful member of NATO, in cyber as well as physical capabilities, but is both constrained by the need to work with its NATO allies and benefits on occasions from their own capabilities, especially in cases where the US may wish to conceal its own operations. Thus there have been reports that Dutch intelligence provided the information that allowed Special Investigator Mueller to indict 12 named Russian military intelligence (GRU) officers for hacking the headquarters of the Democratic National Committee (DNC) during the 2016 Presidential elections, presumably on the basis of Dutch penetration of GRU systems.[88]

This close collaboration with allies extends beyond NATO into smaller and tighter collaborative frameworks. For example the Five Eyes intelligence collaboration between the US, UK, Canada, Australia and New Zealand was established after the Second World War, and essentially is a continuation of the very close intelligence collaboration between these countries during that war ("Five Eyes" refers to the intelligence classification, meaning that documents are to be seen only by officials from these countries). The Five Eyes collaboration has extended into cybersecurity, reinforcing the US' global reach, with Australia a particularly useful collaborator against China. The extent of this collaboration was shown in the documents leaked by Snowden.[89] At a still lower level there is the almost symbiotic relationship between the National Security Agency (NSA) and the Government Communications Head Quarters (GCHQ), the US and British bodies respectively responsible for signals intelligence. Dittmer[90] offers a convincing analysis of the diplomatic assemblages which generated this close collaboration in the struggle to decipher German and Japanese codes during the war and then continued during the Cold War. This collaboration developed to the extent that the two theoretically independent bodies operate almost as one, beyond the control of either the US or UK Governments. Thus the Snowden papers show the NSA getting round the restrictions of the Posse Comitatus legislation in the US by asking GCHQ to operate on their behalf, and vice versa. The author has experience as a British

87 Libicki: *Cyberspace in Peace and War.*
88 https://www.wired.com/story/mueller-indictment-dnc-hack-russia-fancy-bear/.
89 Harding: *The Snowden Files.*
90 Dittmer: *Diplomatic Material.*

Foreign Office official of how GCHQ would routinely use the NSA as the excuse if it did not want to operationalise signals intelligence.

17.3 *US Geopolitical Culture*

The combination of the way in which the US experienced the Internet (geopolitical condition) and the different levels at which the US collaborates with partners (geopolitical fields) help shape the approach of the US to Cyberspace and cybersecurity issues (geopolitical culture). The US sees itself as the responsible operator in Cyberspace, upholding the values (essentially US values) which the Internet originally embodied, and defending them against those who would subvert the Internet for their own purposes. The US only breaks the rules in order to defend the Internet and Cyberspace against those who would do even worse damage (a revealing reflection of traditional US exceptionalism). The US' allies and partners who share the US views of Internet governance and cybersecurity are fellow members of this responsible international community. In a Manichean vision of cybersecurity which reflects President Bush's views after 9/11 (you are either with us or against us), those who question the US approach to Internet governance, or who use Cyberspace for disruption or espionage operations against the US and its allies (so far there have been no degeneration operations against the US and its allies) are seen as rogue nations who take advantage of the US' gift to the world to steal US intellectual property or undermine its allies. This in turn creates new geopolitical fields in which the US engages with these rogue nations at the various levels of cyber collaboration we have identified, and with the differing self-identities that correspond to each level. For example, at the global level the US sees itself as the protector and promoter of global liberal values in Cyberspace, against authoritarian regimes that would threaten freedom in Cyberspace and Internet Sovereignty Advocates who would stifle the US' gift to the world within the restraints of international organisations. At the NATO level, the US becomes the more powerful ally, helping other NATO members defend themselves against hostile disruption, espionage and information operations.

17.4 *Diplomatic Assemblage of the US*

The US approach to Cyberspace can also be analysed by following Dittmer's[91] lead in constructing a diplomatic assemblage, an assemblage of the actors, frameworks and physical objects, which shape US policy making on Cyberspace. Key factors for including within the assemblage would include the separation of powers (the relations between the Presidency and Congress, but

91 Dittmer: *Diplomatic Material*.

also the Supreme Court in deciding the legality of US cyber operations); the legal framework (in particular Posse Comitatus, which places limits on cyber operations within the US, but also the interpretation of the Laws of Armed Conflict [LOAC] when applied to overseas operations); the role of universities and think tanks in framing debates about cybersecurity and Internet governance; inter-agency conflict and rivalries (especially between the NSA and CIA, and the intelligence agencies and the various cyber units within the armed forces); technicians and Internet engineers; the Internet companies (including their willingness or otherwise to collaborate with Government agencies); telecommunications companies, who build and maintain the Internet infrastructure; foreign agencies that collaborate directly with their US counterparts (eg the GCHQ/NSA relationship); foreign Governments, both allies and rivals; technical capabilities (both in limiting and opening up options); whistle blowers (like Snowden); and the personality and objectives of the President of the day. As Dittmer points out, the relative weight and importance of any given factor in the assemblage can change over time. Thus the risk of whistle blowers revealing sensitive information is likely to be a more important factor in deciding whether to launch cyber operations after the Snowden revelations than before.[92] Inter-agency rivalries may be less important now than before with the primacy of the NSA over other agencies more clearly established.[93] Presidents Bush and, especially, Obama prioritised cybersecurity and other cyber issues, but adopted a cautious approach to cyber operations (as we shall see). President Trump seems relatively uninterested in cybersecurity and has abolished the position of cybersecurity coordinator in the White House.[94]

17.5 *US Behaviour in Cyberspace*

So far there has only been one clear cut degeneration cyber operation with Kinetic effect(there may have been an operation against the North Korean medium range ballistic missile programme, but this remains speculative): the so-called Stuxnet attack against the Iranian nuclear processing plant at Natanz. Although no Government has admitted responsiblity for the operation, it has been widely attributed jointly to the US and Israel.[95] The story is widely known, but illustrates some interesting points about the critical geopolitics of the US. The US under President Bush was looking for a way of undermining

92 Harding: *The Snowden Files*.

93 Kaplan: *Dark Territory*.

94 https://www.politico.com/story/2018/05/15/white-house-eliminates-cyber-adviser-post-542916.

95 Sanger: *The Perfect Weapon*.

Iran's nuclear programme without undertaking military action. A cyber operation was proposed to slow Iran's uranium enrichment programme by damaging the centrifuge's essential to the process. The operation was still under development when it was inherited by the incoming Obama administration. The aim of the operation was to infect the computers operating the centrifuges so that they would speed up and slow down outside their operational parameters, causing them eventually to break, while concealing what was going on from their human operators. The technical details of the operation are beyond the scope of this article (and the intellectual capacities of its author).

The interesting aspect from the point of view of this article were the concerns of President Obama before authorising the operation (supposedly).[96] The first concern was about precision. How precise would the operation be, and how sure could they be that it would engage only with the target? The second concern was with collateral damage. How certain could they be that it would only damage the centrifuges, and would not cause wider damage to Iranian computer systems, or Iranian infrastructure and personnel? The third concern was with secrecy. To what extent could they be certain that the operation could be kept confidential without other states knowing about it or being able to attribute the responsibility for the operation? The final concern was about proliferation. How certain were they that they could keep the worm in the Natanz processing plant, and that it would not spread on the wider Internet. The operation, known as "Olympic Games" was in many ways designed to meet these concerns. In theory it was helped in this by the Natanz computers being air-gapped (not connected to the Internet), although this complicated the operation in other ways. The malicious worm was designed only to operate on the Siemens systems used to control the centrifuges at the Natanz processing plant, to have no effect on any other computer system it might infect and to conceal what it was doing from the human operators of the centrifuges. It was assumed that the air gap would ensure that it would not escape from Natanz. For reasons that remain unclear, this latter proved not to be the case, and the worm escaped into the wider Internet. Although, as per its design, it did no damage, it was identified by computer security experts and dubbed Stuxnet. The reasons for wanting to avoid attribution then became clear. Not only were the computer security experts able to attribute the design of the worm with ever greater confidence to the US Government (as well as the Israelis), they were also able to identify the target, alerting the Iranians to the reason their centrifuges had been failing. It had two further effects: computer experts were able to use the elements of the worm to create

96 Sanger: *The Perfect Weapon.*

new cyber weapons; and the Iranians were encouraged to develop their own cyber capability, which they used in disruption attacks against the Saudi oil company Aramco.

Valeriano et al[97] argue that a state seeking to maintain power will focus on degeneration operations. The Stuxnet attack on the Iranian nuclear programme appears to confirm this insight (although one armed attack with Kinetic effect is a rather small data set to draw conclusions from – it would be more convincing if it could be shown that the serial failures of the North Korean medium range ballistic missile programme resulted from US cyber operations[98]). Valeriano et al do raise the question of whether a state's behaviour in Cyberspace reflect power dynamics or strategic culture, although they lean heavily towards the former. However, the discussion above suggests that concepts of critical geopolitics and diplomatic assemblages may offer a richer interpretation of US behaviour and policy decisions in Cyberspace. Key American actors see themselves as the protector of the original values embodied in Cyberspace, as they see themselves as the defenders of liberal values in physical space. This makes the US Government cautious about taking action that might undermine that position. It does not mean that it will not undertake cyberoperations, including degeneration operations, but that such operations will be tightly targeted and, if possible, kept out of public sight. Unlike other states, the US will not boast about its cyber operations, and will try to conceal the extent of its cyberespionage. It will justify such cyberespionage operations on grounds of both the need to defend its conception (the original conception) of the Internet and to protect the heightened cyber vulnerability of US society and economy, and those of its allies. But the US' vision of its role in Cyberspace make it unlikely that it would engage in cyber disruption operations (unlike allies like Israel) and may be limiting its ability or willingness to carry out cyber information operations.

This account of US cyber operations, drawn largely from Sanger,[99] very much fits with the US' own image of itself as a responsible force for good in Cyberspace. However, the Snowden revelations[100] draw a very different picture of US cyber operations, almost as a rogue operator engaging in massive surveillance and cyberespionage against friends as well as rivals, using close relationships with foreign intelligence services (eg GCHQ) to get round restrictions on spying on its own citizens. This seems to undermine Valeriano et al's

97 Valeriano et al: *Cyber Strategy*.
98 Sanger: *The Perfect Weapon*.
99 Sanger: *Perfect Weapon*.
100 Harding: *The Snowden Files*.

claim that a state seeking to maintain power will focus on degeneration operations, while it is rising powers that focus on cyberespionage. The US has allegedly carried out only one degeneration operation (possibly two if the N Korean medium range ballistic missiles are included, although there is only very circumstantial evidence), while, according to Snowden, it is carrying out continuous espionage and surveillance operations. This reflects a key element in US geopolitical culture, the exceptionalism of "the city upon the hill".[101] The actions of "the city upon the hill" are justified because they are carried out by "the city upon the hill". But, just as in physical space, so in Cyberspace this US exceptionalism risks blowback. Just as Russia has used NATO action in Kosovo to "justify" its seizure of the Crimea, Iran was inspired by Stuxnet to launch extensive disruption operations against Saudi Aramco.[102] However, the key here is how the US experience of the Internet, as its progenitor and donor to the world, "conditions" US reactions to the behaviour of other actors in Cyberspace and both reinforces its exceptionalism and its self-image of the policeman of Cyberspace: the city upon the hill meets Superman.

Dittmer[103] argues that the weight and influence of different elements in the diplomatic assemblage vary over time. New configurations of the assemblage give greater importance in framing policy decisions to different actors or factors. We have seen this recently with the debate in the US over net neutrality. The election of President Trump has seen an increase in the influence over administration thinking of the more traditional telecommunications companies, who have traditionally had strong links to the Republican party, and who believe that net neutrality puts them at an unfair commercial disadvantage, accompanied by a diminution in the influence of the state and non-state actors (for example in the influence of the State Department or key liberal think tanks) concerned about supporting dissidents against authoritarian regimes or reducing the digital divide. Indeed the evisceration of the State Department, and the consequent reduction of its weight as an actor in US diplomatic assemblages, has generally privileged commercial over political factors in decisions about foreign policy. The varying strengths of different elements in the diplomatic assemblage may offer a richer way of interpreting the US decision to abandon net neutrality, and one which makes evident the broader implications for the geopolitics of the US in Cyberspace. It remains to be seen whether these include a re-positioning of the US closer to the Internet Sovereignty Advocates.

101 John Winthrop's lecture at Holyrood Church, Southampton, England 21 March 1630.
102 Shaun Riordan: *Cyberdiplomacy*.
103 Dittmer: *Diplomatic Material*.

18 Russia

18.1 *Russia's Experience of Cyberspace*

Russia's experience of the Internet and Cyberspace, and especially that of the Russian state, was very different to that of the US. The emergence of the Internet coincided with the collapse of the Soviet Union ("a major geopolitical disaster of the century" as President Vladimir Putin described it[104]) and the chaos of the Yeltsin years. Many Russians felt humiliated and resented the triumphalism of the US and its allies. The Russian Government watched with alarm the expansion of NATO and the EU into former Warsaw Pact countries and then into former Soviet Republics. In this context, the Internet and Cyberspace were experienced in different ways by different parts of Russian society. Far from a liberating factor or the opportunity to promote values, the Internet became associated with post-Soviet humiliation and US hegemony. For the Russian Government the Internet was experienced as a foreign and alien creation and an existential threat to the Russian state itself. Very early on, the FSB (successor to the KGB focused primarily on internal security) sought to adapt the existing SORM system of phone tapping to the Internet, attaching SORM black boxes to all Internet service providers (ISPs) allowing them to monitor and listen in on Internet traffic.[105] As of 2014 they were still there. The paranoia of the Government about the threat from the Internet increased as journalists and critics of the Government, frozen out of the traditional media by the Government, increasingly took to online blogs, which the Government had more difficulty in closing down. The Government responded by creating its own blogs and encouraging trolls to undermine independent bloggers, putting in place the techniques it would later deploy against western Governments and societies.[106]

The Russian Government's experience of the Internet and Cyberspace was international as well as domestic. It watched with concern as Cyberspace, and especially social media, played a key role in the colour revolutions in the Ukraine and Georgia, and the Arab Spring. It did not distinguish between western public diplomacy and information operations designed to overthrow regimes with which Moscow had maintained good relations or, in the case of Ukraine and Georgia, where Moscow believed it had key national interests at

104 https://www.politifact.com/punditfact/statements/2014/mar/06/john-bolton/did-vladimir-putin-call-breakup-ussr-greatest-geop/.

105 Andrei Soldatov and Irina Borogan: *Red Web: The Kremlin's Wars on the Internet*, Public Affairs, 2017.

106 Soldatov et al: *Red Web*.

stake. This encouraged the idea in Moscow that the West, and especially the US, was weaponizing the Internet as an instrument to undermine and ultimately bring down the Russian regime. This not only reinforced the regime's determination to control the Internet domestically, placing it, alongside China, firmly in the Internet Sovereignty Advocates on Internet governance, but also showed it the possibilities of weaponizing Cyberspace, and particularly information in Cyberspace, as part of its own foreign policy.

Not only was the Russian Government's experience of the Internet very different from that of the American Government, but the experience of Russian citizens was very different from that of US citizens. Firstly, far fewer Russian citizens had access to the Internet in the 90s than in the US, and those who did were soon aware of how much it was monitored by the FSB (indeed many, having grown up in the Soviet Union, would have assumed that any communications were monitored). Those who did have access to the Internet tended to regard it not as a space to be explored and in which they could develop social networks, but as a tool to achieve specific objectives. Thus, as we have seen, journalists and Government critics, driven out of the traditional media by Government and/or oligarch pressure, took to the Internet to write blogs or create online newspapers.[107] In the criminalised society of Yeltsin's Russia,[108] it was inevitable that criminals too would take to the Internet and operate in Cyberspace. With little danger of arrest at home, and often operating from various former Soviet Republics, Russian online criminals[109] developed a range of cybercrime techniques, from straight forward bank robberies to fraud and ransomware attacks (freezing victims computers and then demanding payment in bitcoins to unfreeze it and release the victim's data, as in the Wannacry attack which affected UK hospitals among many other thousands of victims worldwide in 2017). Thus the Russian experience of the Internet, as something foreign imposed from outside, has encouraged Russians to instrumentalise it. Cyberspace is not an area for engagement and interaction, but rather a domain in which Internet tools are developed to pursue specific objectives, whether political or criminal.

18.2 *Russia's Geopolitical Fields*

Toal[110] analyses the interlocking geopolitical fields in which Russia is engaged in Georgia and Ukraine. A similar analysis can be made of Russia's engage-

107 Soldatov et al: *Red Web.*

108 Mark Galeotti: *The Vory: Russia's Super Mafia*, Yale University Press, 2018.

109 https://www.wired.com/2017/03/russian-hacker-spy-botnet/.

110 Toal: *Near Abroad.*

ment with Cyberspace. Firstly there is the domestic space. Here the Russian Government engages with bloggers and dissidents seeking to undermine and marginalise them. It is here that the Russian state has developed the techniques that it has later deployed abroad. The Russian state sees many, if not all, of these "dissident activities" as western inspired, so this is also a space where the state seeks to protect itself from western "attempts to undermine", while trying to create a separate Russian identity, a "Russian exceptionalism", to minimise western political or social influence. This has led to a deployment of a range of different identities, from "Mother Russia" and the Orthodox church to Eurasianism.[111] The lack of apparent consistency and coherence in this "political technology" is another forerunner of later external operations. This internal space is also the political space where the different political factions around Putin interact with each other, and also with the oligarchs and criminal elements. There is considerable evidence of collaboration in particular between the siloviki (elements from the various security agencies) and organised crime.[112] This extends into Cyberspace, where online bank robbers like Slavik appear to have secured protection from arrest by collaborating with the security agencies, combining criminal operations with intelligence gathering operations.[113] This has led some to talk of a siloviki-criminal symbiosis in Cyberspace.[114]

The second geopolitical field in which Russia engages in Cyberspace is what the Russian Government calls its near-abroad (*blizhneye zarubezhye* – the former Soviet republics which declared their independence after the collapse of the Soviet Union). As Toal argues, this is a more complicated space than much western analysis allows.[115] In one sense it is a simple post-colonial relationship between the ex-imperial power (Russia) and the ex-colonies (former Soviet Republics). But within many of the ex-Soviet republics are ethnic Russian minorities, who regard the new post-Soviet states as oppressors and look to Russia for protection. At the same time, the new ex-Soviet Republics look to Europe and the US for confirmation of their democratic identity and support against Russia. Russia sees itself as a protector of the ethnic Russian minorities. But, sensitive to what it sees as NATO's aggressive penetration of its "zone of influence", it also sees itself as resisting further incursions while re-asserting influence, if not control, over its "strategic backyard". These

111 Charles Clover: *Black Wind, White Snow: The Rise of Russia's New Nationalism*, Yale University Press, 2017.
112 Mark Galeotti: *The Vory*.
113 https://www.wired.com/2017/03/russian-hacker-spy-botnet/.
114 Klimburg: *The Darkening Web*.
115 Toal: *Near Abroad*.

complex relationships with the near abroad shaped Russia's engagement with Cyberspace. We have already discussed the 2007 DDOS attack on Estonia following the Estonian Government's decision to move a statue celebrating the Soviet "liberation" of Estonia. The interesting feature was the use of "patriotic hackers" to distance the Kremlin from the operation, allowing a kind of plausible deniability, as seen by Russia at least. Cyber operations accompanied both the war in Georgia in 2008 and the seizure of the Crimea and destabilisation of Eastern Ukraine in 2014.[116] A steady rhythm of cyber operations has been maintained against Ukraine since then, including two operations to take down, temporarily, its electricity grid.[117]

The third geopolitical field is constituted by Russia's relations with Europe and the US (there is a wider geopolitical field constituted by Russia's relations with China and the wider world, but so far this has not shaped significantly Russia's behaviour in Cyberspace). This third field is shaped by Russian resentment at its "humiliation" by the west following the fall of the Soviet Union and its conviction (contested by the West) that NATO and the EU broke commitments made at the time of German re-unification not to expand into former Warsaw Pact, let alone former Soviet, countries. But it is also shaped by Russia's perception that the West consciously used digital technologies and social media to support the colour revolutions, the Arab Spring and Maidan, and are using them in support of dissidents to undermine the Russian regime itself. Seen from the Kremlin, interference in the 2016 US elections is pay back for US interference in the 2014 Russian presidential elections. What is interesting is how Russia used the techniques which evolved in their cyber conflict in the first two geopolitical fields to develop their approach to the third field. It is also clear how the behaviour of the Russian state in all three geopolitical fields has been shaped by Russian experiences of the Internet and Cyberspace, at both individual and state level.

18.3 *Discontinuities between Russia and the Soviet Union*

Valeriano et al[118] argue that Russian operations in Cyberspace are affected by established practices that have carried over from the Soviet period, especially the preference for operating with and through third parties (hence the siloviki-criminal symbiosis) and the priority given to deception operations (*maskirovka*). This forms part of a broader view that sees a continuation of Soviet and strategy and doctrine in current Russian thinking and practice,

116 Klimburg: *The Darkening Web.*
117 Sanger: *The Perfect Weapon.*
118 Valeriano et al: *Cyber Strategy.*

both in Russian military practice and in information operations in Cyberspace (what Soviet doctrine called active measures). There is inevitably some continuity. Many senior figures in both the military and the security agencies began their careers during the Cold War, including of course Putin. Recent writing on Russian military doctrine[119] argues that the concept of violence must include economic, political, religious, ideological, psychological and cultural violence. This insistence on pursuing conflict in all domains in a strategic unity could come straight from a Soviet military manual.

But there are differences, especially in Cyberspace. Firstly ideology: the Soviet Union had an ideology which, theoretically at least, it wished to impose on the world. This limited the nations, organisations or individuals that the Soviet Union could operate with. Unless it was using false flag intelligence operations, for example, the Soviet Union could not cooperate with or co-opt right wing individuals or organisations. Putin's Russia has no such ideological constraints. Because it has no consistent ideology of its own, other than opposition to US hegemony and the liberal world order (at least until it is re-admitted, on its own terms, as a member), Russia can work with, and finance, groups on both left or right. This ideological flexibility is an asset in information operations in Cyberspace, as will be discussed later.

The second major difference is strategy. The Soviet Union was plan driven, whether in the domestic economy, foreign policy or the military. Plans were laid down and strategies developed to achieve the key objectives (even if the objectives were rarely achieved). This made the Soviet Union very strategic, but also rigid and inflexible, unable to react with agility to rapidly changing environments (as seen during its collapse). Putin's Russia appears far less plan-driven and less strategic, particularly in Cyberspace. It is not clear that there were specific plans or strategies to secure Brexit or the election of Trump. These were bonuses. The aim of the information operations in both cases was to generate chaos and destabilisation of UK and US political debate. The Russian seizure of the Crimea (pace Bolton) was not a long planned operation to re-assert Russian authority in its near abroad, but rather a tactical reaction to the new Ukrainian Government and the danger that it might enter NATO (threatening the Russian naval base at Sebastopol).[120] Recent Russian military writing talks about controlling or managing chaos.[121] The suggestion seems to be that Russia, particularly in Cyberspace, seeks to generate chaos and

119 Gudrun Persson: *The War of the Future*, Russian Studies (NATO Defense College) 03/17 July 2017.

120 Toal: *Near Abroad*.

121 Persson: *The War of the Future*.

destabilisation confident that it is better able to navigate the consequent complexities than its rivals. The comparison between Soviet doctrine and Russian chaos theory is reminiscent of the world championship chess matches between the Russian Soviet Grandmaster Botvinnik and Latvian Soviet Grandmaster in the early 1960s.[122] Botvinnik was a classical player, focused on planning and strategy, and darling of the Soviet establishment. Tal, something of an outsider, preferred provoking tactical complexities, confident that he could better navigate his way through them, both tactically and psychologically. Often his sacrifices were unsound, as was discovered in subsequent analysis, but such was the tactical and psychological pressure that his opponents were unable to navigate safely to harbour.

18.4 *Russian Operations in Cyberspace*

Valeriano et al[123] also argue that a state in decline prefers disruption operations to other kinds of cyber operations. Implicitly they are referring to Russia. There is considerable supporting evidence: including Russian disruption operations against Estonia, Georgia and Ukraine. Even when Russia launches an intelligence gathering operation, the intelligence is subsequently used for disruption. The hack of the Democrat National Committee (DNC) during the 2016 Presidential Election Campaign appears to be a classic example.[124] Officers from the GRU (Russian Military Intelligence), subsequently indicted by special counsel Robert Mueller, hacked the computer systems of the DNC stealing data, including emails between John Podesta and Democrat candidate Hillary Clinton. The emails were passed to Wikileaks, who released selected emails during the campaign without revealing their provenance. In this case the GRU used a cyberespionage operation to acquire information that was then leaked to the public to disrupt and influence the US presidential election, what Valeriano et al call "acquire-release-spread". The "spread" was guaranteed by releasing the emails through Wikileaks, which at that stage still enjoyed considerable credibility, and which allowed the Russians to distance themselves from the operation.

Even though such examples seem to support Valeriano's structural argument in the case of Russia, there is still evidence that it is overly deterministic, and fails to take account of how Russia sees its itself in Cyberspace. To start with, it is not clear that Putin's Russia sees itself as a state in decline. Russia is certainly in decline in comparison with the might of the Soviet Union at

122 Mikhail Tal: *The Life and Games of Mikhail Tal*, Everyman Chess, 1997.
123 Valriano et al: *Cyber Strategy*.
124 Sanger: *The Perfect Weapon*.

its height. But in comparison with Yeltsin's Russia of the 1990s, Putin could plausibly argue that Russia is a country that has recovered and is even on the rise. While its economy remains small, and overly dependent on oil and gas exports, it has modernised its military capabilities and demonstrated the ability to project power in the Middle East and, arguably, in Cyberspace. Secondly, Valeriano et al's structural approach does not take account of the specific events and trends which have led Russia to adopt its more disruption based approach to cyber operations, in particular its perceived need to assert its authority in its "near abroad", both to protect Russian communities there and to undermine western influence, and its consequent confrontation with the EU and the US. The various disinformation and misinformation techniques with which Russia tries to destabilise societies in its near abroad and the west were initially developed and honed in the national sphere to undermine critics of the Putin regime. Russia indeed claims that it is responding only to the efforts of the west to undermine Russia's authority in its strategic hinterland, and in Russia itself. Russian Chief of Staff Gerasimov's famous article,[125] which some have seen as a statement of Russian hybrid warfare doctrine, in fact seeks to respond to what he regards as western hybrid warfare. Gerasimov argues that the west has developed a new form of hybrid warfare, combining military and economic activity with public diplomacy campaigns, digital means, including social media, and support for dissidents to overthrow regimes it disapproves of. Western hybrid warfare combines the activities of Governments with economic entities and NGOs in coherent strategies, which can be seen at work in the colour revolutions and the Arab Spring. Russia must develop its own capacities for hybrid warfare so that it can take on the West at its own game. Gerasimov may vastly overestimate the west's capacity for strategic action, and mistake standard public diplomacy for covert attempts at regime change. However, public diplomacy in authoritarian regimes is problematic. If the rationale for public diplomacy is that it aims to influence foreign publics so that they can influence the decisions of their Governments, why do public diplomacy in authoritarian regimes where the Government pays no attention to public opinion, unless as part of regime change? Be that as it may, the key here is that Gerasimov, and the Russian leadership in general, see their actions in Cyberspace as reactions to Western actions designed to undermine the Putin regime. This fits with the critical geopolitical analysis above.

125 file:///C:/Users/win/Documents/Geopolitics%20of%20Cyberspace/MilitaryReview_20160228_art008.pdf.

18.5 *Russian Cyber (Mis) Information Operations*

It may be worth quickly looking at Russian information operations (in Russian doctrine, "information warfare", which must always accompany, and precede, military warfare, includes cyber operations as well as other non cyber disinformation and misinformation activities) to explore to what extent they reflect Russia's geopolitical culture and conditions, and to what extent a diplomatic assemblage could be usefully constructed. Firstly Russian information[126] operations against the US and European countries have no specific positive objective. Their aim is to cause confusion and destabilise. They do not want to convince western audiences to believe a given Russian narrative, but rather undermine confidence in all narratives, especially the narratives of western Governments and liberal elites. Secondly, Russian information operations are channelled through surrogates and anonymous or deceptive social media accounts. Given Russia's ideological neutrality, this allows Russian information operations to craft segmented, often contradictory, messages designed to appeal to different segments of western societies. Thirdly, Russian information operations are adept at making use of social media to ensure that their misinformation reaches precisely the echo chambers in western societies most likely to believe it. Russia did not invent the phenomena of echo chambers, whereby people in western societies increasingly listen only to the news and opinions they already agree with, and interact only with people whose prejudices they already share. Nor did the social media companies. However, the algorithms underlying social media platforms, which ensure that users only get adverts and news likely to appeal to them, have reinforced the process.[127] The Russians have understood this early, and have taken advantage of these algorithms to help polarise debate and undermine social and political discourse in western societies.

The Russian experience of the Internet and Cyberspace, initially as a foreign imposition threatening the Russian state, and then as something which could be instrumentalised, underlies Russian cyber information operations. This experience also ties in with resentment against and the belief that they are responding to the west, not initiating conflict. The broader geopolitical culture, with both continuities from and breaches with Soviet doctrines, has shaped how these operations are structured and carried out. The various techniques of trolling, disruption and misinformation were first used in the domestic sphere and then developed further in the near abroad before being unleashed against

126 P W Singer: *LikeWar: The Weaponisation of Social Media*, Eamon Dolan/Houghton Mifflin Harcourt, 2018.

127 Shaun Riordan: *Cyberdiplomacy*.

the US and Europe. This all suggests that critical geopolitics can offer a richer and more nuanced analysis of Russian behaviour in Cyberspace than the structured approach offered by Valeriano etc.

18.6 *Russia's Diplomatic Assemblage*

An alternative approach would be to construct a diplomatic assemblage around Russian engagement in Cyberspace. This would need to include as factors President Putin himself, the various factions, including the siloviki, "working towards him" (in Ian Kershaw's felicitous phrase, although he is referring to Hitler[128]), the relationships and tensions, between the different intelligence/security agencies, especially the FSB and GRU, Russia's cyber capabilities and the opportunities these represents, the physical proximity and access of key actors to the decision-making process, the level of Russia's integration in Cyberspace and the vulnerabilities this opens up, commercial/economic interests and their vulnerability to western counter-measures, criminal gangs and other non-state cyber actors and their relations with the siloviki, NGOs and civil society active in Russia, Russian minorities in the near abroad, and their relations with the Governments where they live, the Russian military and the western states and their attitudes towards Russia (as interpreted in Moscow). As Dittmer[129] points out, the relative importance of each of these factors varies over time as different configurations of the assemblage emerge and then disappear. Thus the rise in prominence of the GRU in recent years is likely to lead to increased tension with the FSB. Perceived weakness in the EU or public disinterest in the US may encourage more aggressive approaches to Cyberspace, especially among rival elites competing for the President's favour. Conversely a perceived threat of further sanctions in retaliation for cyber operations may strengthen the hand of commercial interests in moderating cyber operations. A key point that emerges from both the critical geopolitics and diplomatic assemblage analyses is the importance of understanding other actors in their own terms. This does not mean accepting those terms, but seeing the world from their point of view. As diplomats know, but politicians often forget, empathy is not the same as sympathy.

128 Ian Kershaw: *Hitler 1936–1945: Nemesis*, Allen Lane, 2001.

129 Dittmer: *Diplomatic Material*.

19 China

19.1 *China's Experience of Cyberspace*

In many ways China's experience of Cyberspace was similar to Russia's. The Internet was seen as alien and a threat to the domestic hegemony of the Government and, especially, the Communist Party. But in the 1990s China was still relatively weak and in the process of opening up its economy to world markets. It could not simply reject the Internet and cut itself off from Cyberspace, all the more so as the Internet increasingly drove the process of economic globalisation. There was also a difference between Russia and China's experience of Cyberspace. China in the 1990s may have still been economically weak, but it had a roadmap already set out for its growth. It was not as chaotic as Yeltsin's Russia, with far more political and social control, and therefore less scope for the development of organised crime separate from the Party and Government. This was even more true after the Tiananmen incident, which the Chinese authorities used as a pretext to crack down on the black market and organised crime. This meant that a semi-autonomous organised cybercrime did not develop in China. Rather than the symbiotic relationship between the siloviki and criminals that developed in Russia, Chinese intelligent services encouraged young hackers to penetrate Internet systems and troll from patriotic motives. Furthermore, as China was looking with confidence to a future world order in which it would be a key player, it had less interest in destabilising the existing world order, from which its economic development was benefiting.

China's particular experience of Cyberspace focuses on different elements or concerns. It is not only that China sees the Internet as an alien, US creation, but that China fears US hegemony in Cyberspace, and the constraints that may impose on China's development. To the extent that China is freely integrated into the global Internet, it fears US efforts to undermine domestic security. But it is not only the concern about activities by the US and other western Governments. Since the 1989 Tiananmen demonstrations, China has maintained a firm control over political dissidence, ensuring strict adherence to the official account of the events. It fears that independent sources of information, whether entering China on or off line, could undermine the Government and the party line, as well as the credibility of their political and social discourse in general. The Chinese Government has responded to the danger in two ways. Firstly it created the "Great Firewall of China" to cut off access to "dangerous websites" like western social media platforms and independent news media. It backed this up by encouraging the development of parallel Chinese social media platforms, which would be firmly under the control of the Communist

Party and more easily monitored for subversive posts. In effect it began the move towards a separate Chinese Internet, establishing Chinese sovereignty in Cyberspace. Secondly, it recruited young Chinese Internet users to troll subversive posts and promote Chinese Government positions, the so-called wumaobang (fifty cent gangs[130]). Unlike Russia's use of "patriotic" hackers to attack foreign countries (eg in Estonia in 2007), the wumaobang targeted possible dissent at home.

Chinese concerns also centred on the technology gap with the US. The establishment of the Internet by the US, and its domination of the protocols and standards regulating it, reinforced the perception of China's low technological levels compared with the US and the need to close the gap. Given the unlikelihood that the US would simply share sensitive technology with what it increasingly saw as a commercial rival, this led to cyberespionage on a massive scale, as Chinese hackers stole intellectual property from the US and its western allies. But as China made use of the stolen intellectual property to develop its own technological capacities, it also realised the potential of these technologies to collect data about, and maintain surveillance of, Chinese citizens. This has led to the development of the Social Credit System, whereby all Chinese citizens will receive a social credit rating based on their on- and offline behaviour, and which will decide access to employment, benefits and even the development of their private life.[131]

19.2 *China's Geopolitical Culture*

China's geopolitical culture can only be understood in the context of the country's name in Chinese, and the Communist Party's interpretation of Chinese history. "China" is a western name for China derived from the Qin dynasty. It is unrelated to the Chinese name for the country, Zhongguo (中国), which is captured when westerners refer to the Middle Kingdom. A better translation would be the central country, the country at the centre of the international system. Historically China saw itself at the centre between Tianshang (天上 – heaven) and Tianxia (天下 – earth), with the emperor mediating relations between the two. More mundanely, the emperor sat at the centre of a tributary network of relations with other states. This has two implications for the analysis of China's interactions with both physical and Cyberspace. Firstly, China historically has no concept of international relations in the European

130 Segal: *The Hacked World War.*

131 https://www.wired.co.uk/article/chinese-Government-social-credit-score-privacy-invasion.

sense. Secondly, if President Trump's ambition is to "make America great again (MAGA)", President Xi Jinping's ambition is to "make China Zhonguo again".

The European concept of international relations originates in the contingencies of European history. Despite the efforts of a succession of would be hegemons, no single European state was ever able to establish hegemony over the European continent. The result was continuous competition between a range of European states, all enjoying theoretically equal status. A series of treaties from Westphalia via Utrecht to the Concert of Vienna progressively set the rules of the game for this competition between different states or nations, from which were derived European concepts of international relations, international law and diplomacy (if international relations describes the relationships between states of equal status, diplomats are needed to manage those relationships). These European concepts of international relations, international law and diplomacy were subsequently imposed on the rest of the world, initially by European imperial expansion then by US global hegemony. As the latter declines in the transition to a multipolar world, we can expect to see other traditions' and cultures' alternative perspectives on how to manage the international system[132]

The Chinese historical experience is very different. The Han early established their hegemony over most of what we now call China. Rather than conflicts between states of equal status, Chinese history centres around a series of centralising dynasties, with shorter or longer periods of chaos and civil war when dynasties collapse, and before a new one is established. China has never recognised other states as of equal status, but rather as subordinates in China's system for managing the external world. These "tributary" states paid tribute to the emperor (in effect recognising his suzerainty or over-lordship) in return for the benefits of being part of the Chinese system. The cultural clash between the Chinese tributary system and the Western system of international relations is well illustrated by the visit to China by Lord Macartney in 1793-4, and his failure to secure trading relations between the British and Chinese empires.[133] From a Chinese point of view both international relations and diplomacy are western concepts imposed on China at a time of Chinese weakness in the 19th and 20th century. For example, the first Foreign Ministry in China, the Zongli Yamen (总理衙门) was only created in 1861 to be replaced by the Waiwubu (外務部 – external relations department) in 1901, on both occasions at western insistence and following western military intervention. Thus for China, the

132 Oliver Stuenkel: *Post Western World*, Polity, 2016.

133 Henry Kissinger: *On China*, Penguin, 2011.

international relations system and concept of diplomacy are as much western inventions and impositions as the Internet.

President Xi Jinping wants to "Make China Zhonguo" again, return China to its position at the centre of its own international system. In other words, China does not necessarily want to compete with the west in the existing international system, but create its own parallel system centred on Beijing. The main manifestation of this desire to return China to the centre is the construction of the New Silk Roads, or Belt Road Initiative (BRI). Although ostensibly a plan to construct infrastructure linking China through Central Asia to Europe, its real purpose is geopolitical. Combined with the Asian Infrastructure Investment Bank (AIIB), the BRI is part of a strategy to return China to the centre of its own political and economic system. This combines with the Chinese Communist Party's interpretation of history and President Xi Jinping's own re-ordering of Chinese politics.

It is sometimes argued in the west that the Chinese Communist Party (CCP) justifies its position in power through a guarantee to the Chinese people of economic growth and social stability. While it is certainly true that it is concerned about the consequences for social stability (and its own position in power) of an economic slowdown, this is only part of the story. More fundamentally, the CCP argues that it alone was capable of rescuing China from the century of humiliation it suffered following its first engagement with the modern West at the end of the 18th century. This provides a more immediate political reason for re-establishing China as a major power. In as far as Cyberspace offers new opportunities for establishing China as a major power and as the centre of its own system, Chinese geopolitical culture will dictate that it should be used in that way.

Xi Jinping's personal ambitions also feed into the equation. Former leader Deng Xiaoping laid down the principles for interpreting China's past (including the century of humiliation) and for China's political development and engagement with the world.[134] In terms of history this meant accepting that Mao made mistakes and disowning the Great Leap Forward and the Cultural Revolution. In terms of political development and engagement with the outside world this meant a time limited collective leadership at home and keeping a low profile abroad. Xi has overturned all these principles.[135] The Great Leap Forward and Cultural Revolution are no longer seen as mistakes, but as necessary steps towards the re-emergence of China as a great power. Xi has created his own personal leadership of the country and party and abolished

134 Alexander V Pantsov: *Deng Xiaoping: A Revolutionary Life*, Oxford University Press, 2017.

135 Kerry Brown: *CEO, China: The Rise of Xi Jinping*, I B Tauris, 2017.

the term limits on the senior leadership, creating the possibility for himself of leadership for life. Abroad he has pursued a high profile, combining the Belt Road Initiative with an aggressive assertion of China's sovereignty claims in the South China Sea. To secure his position at home he has, under the pretext of an anti-corruption campaign, carried out the most brutal purge of the CCP since the Cultural Revolution, while repressing dissidents, criticism of the CCP and ethnic minorities. The combination of China's geopolitical culture and Xi's recreation of the personality cult of the leader shape China's engagement with Cyberspace.

19.3 *Chinese Concepts of Deterrence*

Libicki[136] argues for a distinction between what he describes as "blue" and "red" deterrence. He ascribes blue deterrence to the US and red deterrence to China. Blue deterrence focuses on stated rules which it seeks to uphold. It assumes the ability to punish other states for breaking those rules, and the willingness to do so in the face of possible counter reprisals. Red deterrence focuses on power, and especially the relative hierarchy of power among states. Red deterrence is not aimed at maintaining obedience to the rules, but rather maintaining the state's position (at the top) of the global power hierarchy. In the terms of a sinologist, red deterrence is more about maintaining face than maintaining international stability. To the extent that Libicki is right, and separate Chinese documents on deterrence in Cyberspace suggest that he may be,[137] the distinction between blue and red deterrence reflects the different historical experience and geopolitical cultures of the US and China. Chinese political culture does not order the world on the basis of equal status among states, but as a hierarchy of states based on relative power. The Chinese experience of history sees the international state system not as a natural order of things, but as a creation of the west in which China had no say because of its "humiliation" at the hands of the west at the time. Unlike the interpretation of western commentators, China aims not to rise, but to return to its natural position at the centre.

19.4 *China's Geopolitical Fields*

Like the other countries that we have examined, China operates in multiple geopolitical fields. Like Russia, China's first, and most important, geopolitical field in Cyberspace has been domestic. As we have seen, the Internet was

136 Libicki: *Cyberspace in Peace and War*.

137 https://www.reddragon1949.com/chinese-military-views-中國軍事觀/chinese-military-analysis-of-cyber-space-deterrence-important-strategic-points-淺析網絡空間威懾的特徵、/.

experienced as a US imposition and a threat to both the Government and the CCP. The Great Firewall of China, the development of Chinese equivalents of Western Internet companies and social media platforms and the Social Credit Scheme have allowed the Chinese authorities to assert control over Cyberspace in China, to the extent that some commentators in the west have begun to speculate on the break up of the Internet.[138] In many ways, the Internet in China seems to operate in very different ways to the rest of the world. The focus on maintaining control over the Internet at home has led to China being a fervent supporter of cyber sovereignty in debates about Internet governance. Although China's concept of cyber sovereignty has not been formally defined, in essence it affirms that sovereign nations should be granted control over networks and data within their borders to manage as they see fit.[139] Xi Jinping has argued that the "Chinese model" "is a new option for nations who want to speed up their development while protecting their independence".[140] This applies as much to cyber as to physical space. As we have seen, unlike Russia, China has, in general, not deployed cyber information and disruption operations abroad. Rather it has preferred to deploy such techniques at home, using the wumaobang (五毛党 – fifty cent army) or patriotic trollers to drown China's social media platforms in nationalistic and pro-Government posts.

Given the Chinese Government's and the CCP's experience of the Internet as a US imposed existential threat, it is unsurprising that there is a confrontation in Cyberspace with the US. From the very beginning China has been concerned about US hegemony in Cyberspace, and has sought to undermine it.[141] This has played out in the Chinese challenge to US Internet governance models. It has led China to propose, as part of a digital silk road (of which more below) to propose the development of optic fibre cables directly linking China with Europe, and thus avoiding data passing through US cables (which could amount to a further step in the break up of a global Internet). Above all, China's experience of a technology gap with the US has led it to focus its cyber operations on the massive theft of intellectual property, especially relating to digital military technologies, from the US. This massive theft of intellectual property has fed through into tensions in China's relations with the

138 https://www.nytimes.com/2018/10/15/opinion/Internet-google-china-balkanization.html.

139 https://www.hoover.org/sites/default/files/research/docs/segal_chinese_cyber_diplomacy.pdf.

140 https://jamestown.org/program/cyber-sovereignty-and-the-prcs-vision-for-global-Internet-governance/.

141 Libicki: *Cyberspace in Peace and War*.

US in physical space, while the physical confrontation in the South China Sea threatens to feed through into Cyberspace.

The final geopolitical field where China operates in Cyberspace is the new Silk Road. As we have seen, the Belt and Road Initiative (BRI) is an essential part of the CCP's and Xi Jinping's strategy to make China Zhongguo again. The infrastructure on offer is not only physical, but also digital and telecommunications. China is seeking to create a digital, or information, silk road through cross-border optical cables, other communication trunk line networks, transcontinental submarine optical cable projects and spatial (satellite) communications.[142] This combines with the "China model" outlined above – technological/economic development while protecting independence – which has significant attractions for many countries, especially authoritarian ones, along the route of the terrestrial and maritime silk roads. The flip side is that membership of the digital silk road implies support for China's demands for a "multilateral democratic and transparent" global Internet governance system.[143]

19.5 *Chinese Behaviour in Cyberspace*

Valeriano et al[144] argue that a rising power would be likely to focus on espionage rather than disruption. To a large extent China seems to follow this. Concerned about the technology gap and the US' hegemony in Cyberspace, China's cyber operations have focused almost entirely on espionage. This has mainly been targeted at stealing intellectual property, especially from the US, although Chinese hackers have also stolen data about US Government employees.[145] This espionage has undoubtedly helped China close the technology gap, in both digital and military technology. It has also enabled the Chinese Government to set its "Made in China 2025" target to become the world leader in artificial intelligence, computing power and military technology (among other targets – another reflection of "make China Zhongguo again"). However, there are signs that this is changing. Following the US indictment of five Chinese army officers for cyberespionage and the threat of economic sanctions, Presidents Xi Jinping and Obama signed an agreement to reduce cyberespionage between their countries (Xi subsequently signed similar agreements with other western countries). The initial signs were that the agreement was a success, with

142 https://www.hoover.org/sites/default/files/research/docs/segal_chinese_cyber_diplomacy.pdf.

143 https://jamestown.org/program/cyber-sovereignty-and-the-prcs-vision-for-global-Internet-governance/.

144 Valeriano et al: *Cyber Strategy*.

145 Klimburg: *The Darkening Web*.

Chinese cyberespionage operations against the US reducing dramatically up until the end of 2016[146] (there has been recent evidence of a resurgence in these operations, but this may be a response to President Trumps imposition of tariffs on Chinese products). There are various explanations for Xi's decision to reach agreement with Obama: he calculated that the damage economic sanctions would cause would outweigh any benefits China was receiving from cyberespionage; it allowed Xi to centralise and take command of China's chaotic cyber operations (fitting in with the more "imperial" geopolitical culture Xi was seeking to develop); or that China was stealing more intellectual property than it had the capacity to process. But an alternative explanation with interesting implications for diplomacy is that China no longer needed to steal the digital and technology secrets, that China has closed the technology gap to the extent that it can now be self-reliant on its own engineering and technological capacities.

A recent development has been China's entry into the world technology protocols and standards. Such has been the US' lead in digital technologies that virtually all protocols and standards for the operation of these technologies have been set in the US or by US companies. Thus the protocols that enable the Internet to function were established in the US, as were the industry standards that enabled the first four generations of mobile telephones to operate. China seemed to take little interest in such issues, only sending a few technicians, or sometimes a bemused diplomat from the local embassy to take part. This has changed. Now China sends hundreds of technicians and Government representatives to standard setting meetings.[147] The immediate focus is on fifth generation (5G) mobile phones. 5G will roll out in two phases, with the second focusing on connecting mobile phones with other devices and machines (the Internet of Things – IOT). While the technology standards for the first phase remain set largely in the US and Japan, the Chinese technology giant Huawei has put an enormous effort into the second IOT phase. As of now the majority of the technology standards for phase 2 of 5G have been developed in China.[148] The US, rather late in the day, seems to have realised the implications of this, and has launched an international campaign to undermine Huawei's position on security grounds.[149] Nevertheless, China's realisation of the importance of technology and industry standards not only reflects

146 Klimburg: *The Darkening Web*.

147 https://www.hoover.org/sites/default/files/research/docs/segal_chinese_cyber_diplomacy.pdf.

148 www.jefferies.com/CMSFiles/Jefferies.com/files/Insights/TelecomServ.pdf.

149 https://www.ft.com/content/323abb62-f9e1-11e8-af46-2022a0b02a6c.

concerns about the perceived technology gap, but also the geopolitical drive to put China back at the centre of international developments and systems: to make China Zhongguo again.[150]

As China develops it's technological capabilities and integrates its society ever more into the Internet and IOT, it itself become more vulnerable to cyberattack. The Government's main concern is no longer only how to establish cyber sovereignty to maintain control over its population, but also the broader cybersecurity concerns shared by the US and other western countries. This tendency will be strengthened to the extent that China no longer needs cyberespionage to compensate for the perceived technology gap, and feels confident in depending on its own capacities as it moves towards "Made in China 2025". Unlike Russia, China has never been interested in disrupting or destabilising the existing political and economic system. Its economic development has benefited too much from it. Rather it seeks to establish an alternative system, built around the BRI and the AIIB, with Beijing at the centre. Equally in Cyberspace, China does not want to destabilise or disrupt the Internet, but rather construct its own system built around the Digital Silk Road and the concept of cyber sovereignty. China is confident it can attract adherents to both its physical and cyber systems. If Russia and N Korea (and to a lesser degree Iran) continue with their cyber disruption strategies, undermining global cybersecurity, in particular through the siloviki-organised crime symbiosis in Russia, this could bring them into growing conflict with China. China's interest is in cyber stability, but on its terms.

This may create the conditions for greater cyber collaboration between China and the West. China has been concerned that the Russian hacking of the DNC during the 2016 election campaign, and the US response, will accelerate the militarisation of Cyberspace. For some Chinese analysts, growing concerns about the hacking of political parties, fake news and interference with elections points to some shared interests with the west.[151] The increasingly inward looking attitude of the US may create opportunities to play an even larger role in defining the international order in Cyberspace. This may be reinforced if the Trump administration continues to abandon cherished shibboleths of the Free Internet Countries, such as net neutrality. The growing Chinese interest in global interconnectivity may make it more willing to compromise with other like-minded countries and regional groupings focused on cybersecurity and

150 http://thecorner.eu/world-economy/5g-the-real-reason-behind-us-attacks-on-huawei/78010/.

151 https://www.hoover.org/sites/default/files/research/docs/segal_chinese_cyber_diplomacy.pdf.

cyber stability, such as the EU. The next section will therefore look at the EU as a geopolitical actor in Cyberspace.

20 The European Union

The European Union is, of course, not a nation state, but rather a conglomeration of states which combines common policies and objectives at a Union level with political diversity at the member state level. This is particularly true of foreign policy, where attempts to forge a Common Defence and Security Policy (CDSP) have been continually undermined by divergences of interests and policy objectives at the member state level, especially among the larger members. Moreover, the European Union is, to some extent, a historic project in abolishing geopolitics. It may seem strange, therefore, to talk about the geopolitics of the EU's participation in Cyberspace. However, the EU is, and sees itself as, a major player in Cyberspace, at the Union as well as member state level. It will be interesting to see whether the ideas of critical geopolitics can be applied to the EU as an actor in Cyberspace, as they have been with the US, Russia and China.

20.1 *The EU's Experience of Cyberspace*

The EU's experience of Cyberspace is closer to that of the US than that of Russia or China. Although the Internet is seen as a US invention, it has not been experienced as a threat to EU structures or stability. It is not seen as alien, and European Governments and citizens have competed to participate in Cyberspace, whether for commerce, information exchange or leisure. However, there are differences between the EU and US experience. While Cyberspace is not experienced as alien, there are concerns that the Internet and the digital technologies that drive it are overly American. This is reflected by initiatives at both the EU and members states level to encourage the development of indigenous Internet companies and to promote research and development of digital technologies. While these initiatives have enjoyed some limited successes, they have not threatened the US domination of these technologies, or reduced the risk being overtaken by Chinese efforts.

The EU is less concerned than Russia or China by the prospect of US hegemony in Cyberspace. However, it is more concerned about the domination of e-commerce by US companies, and the extent to which that enables them to avoid taxation and regulation. The concern is reinforced by the perception that increasing online purchasing from mainly US online vendors is undermining European high streets and European companies, especially as a series of iconic companies across Europe report financial difficulties. European support for the multi-stakeholder model of Internet governance to some extent reflects the self-image of the EU as a governance experiment. But it does not mean that the EU does not have regulatory concerns, especially about the behaviour of US companies, Internet content and privacy of its citizens' data (a much more important issue in the EU than in the US).

20.2 *EU Geopolitical Culture*

Like the other countries' examined, the EU's geopolitical culture is shaped both by its history, as it interprets it, and by its self-image. The European Economic Community and then the European Union has its origins in the post-World War II determination that Europe should never again wreak such carnage on itself. As the Cold War developed, this combined with the pursuit of economic growth and social development as the non-military corollary to NATO in resisting the Soviet Union. In a sense both roles were negative or passive. Avoiding both a return to Europe's bloody past and the victory of Soviet communism. Following the end of the Cold War and the collapse of the Soviet Union, the European Union adopted a more positive and proactive attitude. It had successfully survived the Cold War, and few foresaw any danger of a return to old nationalisms. Again in collaboration with NATO, it sought to promote "European values" in the former members of the Warsaw Pact and the more European of the former Soviet Republics, supporting the transition to democracy and market economies while handing out the carrot of EU membership. Despite the disaster in the Balkans, where it signally failed to show the capacity to manage an international crisis on its borders, and had to be bailed out by the US, it generally felt satisfied with its performance both externally and internally, as the Euro was launched as the single currency for most of its members.

At the same time, the EU began to think of itself, and talk about itself, as a unique experiment in political organisation, a foretaste of where international politics would go in the 21st century. This was captured by Robert Cooper's division of states into pre-modern, modern and post-modern.[152] Although Cooper denies that he saw an inevitable historical progression from one kind of state to another, his claim is undermined by the language he used. In the pre-modern world the state does not enjoy a monopoly on violence, criminal and other gangs roam free and chaos roams. The modern state is characterised by "the recognition of state sovereignty and the consequent separation of

152 Robert Cooper: *The Breaking of Nations: Order and Chaos in the Twenty-First Century*, Atlantic Books, 2003.

domestic affairs, with a prohibition on external interference in the former".[153] The external relations of modern states are managed primarily by the balance of power. The post-modern state does not rely on the balance of power to manage its external relations, nor does it affirm the separation of domestic and foreign affairs. Rather than asserting its sovereignty, it sees the advantages of pooling it with other like-minded countries. Instead of a coercive diplomacy backed up by military force, it pursues a normative diplomacy based around rules and norms of behaviour, confident in the attractiveness of its model to win over other countries. Although Cooper was writing in the same period of Cold War euphoria which produced Fukuyama's End of History, he clearly had the EU in mind as the first and, at that point, only post-modern state. The EU eagerly adopted the concept, which fitted well with its self-image as a radical political experiment. Confident that the world was moving in its direction, the EU's geopolitical culture led it into a normative diplomacy based on rule of law, in both physical and Cyberspace.

The EU's self-identification as a post-modern state, and political experiment, is reflected in its 2013 Cybersecurity Strategy.[154] The objectives of this strategy include the promotion of the openness and freedom of the Internet, encouraging efforts to develop norms of behaviour, the application of existing international law in Cyberspace, the closure of the digital divide and the participation in international efforts to build a cybersecurity capacity. All of these objectives reflect the EU's geopolitical culture and self-identification as a postmodern state. The EU's approach to trying to achieve them would be based around a normative diplomacy leveraging the EU's attractiveness as an online market.

20.3 *The EU's Geopolitical Fields*

The geopolitical fields in which the EU operates in Cyberspace are reflected in, and can be explored through, the EU's strategic cyber partnerships, through which it seeks to implement the strategy and secure its normative objectives. Renard[155] suggests that these strategic partnerships should be analysed at the reflexive, relational and structural levels. At the reflexive level, these strategic partnerships are integrative in that they generate more cohesion and coherence in EU foreign policy. The EU uses cyber partnerships with non-EU members to forge EU cyber policy above the heads, and wishes, of the member

153 Robert Cooper: *The Breaking of Nations.*
154 http://eeas.europa.eu/archives/docs/policies/eu-cyber-security/cybsec_comm_en.pdf.
155 http://www.egmontinstitute.be/content/uploads/2018/01/EPS-EU-cyber-partners_RENARD_AM.pdf?type=pdf.

states. They are also positional, in the sense that they seek to affirm the EU as a global player. At the relational level, the partnerships are a means of managing relationships, but also of socialising non-EU members into the normative and rule-based culture of the EU. At a structural level, the partnerships serve as an instrument to promote and shape a more effective multilateral system. It is interesting that, as a "postmodern" state, the EU's geopolitical fields are less geographical and more conceptual.

20.4 *EU Behaviour in Cyberspace*

The EU's approach to Cyberspace has enjoyed some successes. The Budapest Convention on Cybercrime, often called simply the Budapest Convention, was signed in Budapest in 2001 and has now been ratified by 61 nations. The Convention was the first international treaty to address Internet crime by harmonising national laws, improving investigative techniques and increasing international cooperation. However, its effectiveness has been undermined by those countries, and major powers in Cyberspace, which have not signed it and which include Russia, China and India. The Global Alliance Against Child Sexual Abuse Online was launched by the European Commission, in coordination with the US, in 2012. It subsequently merged with the British initiative We Protect to create the We Protect Global Alliance to End Child Sexual Exploitation Online.[156] The focus on cybercrime, rather than the more military aspects of cybersecurity, reflects both the civilian nature of the European Commission (the more military aspects are covered by NATO's Tallinn Manual) and the normative, "post-modern" geopolitical culture of the EU.

However, the EU's approach to Cyberspace has also encountered significant setbacks. It has not found a successful way of countering massive Chinese cyberespionage, especially in relation to the theft of intellectual property. If it has made progress on this it is only on the tailcoats of President Obama's negotiation with Xi Jinping. Nor has it been able to develop an effective response to Russian disruption and information operations. In the case of Russian disruption operations in Estonia in 2007, Tallinn sought support from NATO rather than the EU. But Russian interference in the Brexit referendum and attempts to interfere in French and German elections show that these are political as well as security issues. The EU has established the East Stratcom Task Force to combat Russian disinformation campaigns in the Eastern neighbourhood. However, it is not clear how effective it is, and it does not tackle Russian information operations within the EU itself. It also reflects a weakness in the

156 https://ec.europa.eu/home-affairs/what-we-do/policies/organized-crime-and-human-trafficking/global-alliance-against-child-abuse_en.

EU's approach to its external relations in general, derived from its self-image as the only "post-modern" state. So convinced is the Task Force that it is right and the, primarily Russian, information output is wrong that it tends to adopt a black and white approach that undermines its effectiveness.

The Snowden revelations about US cyber surveillance operations, and in particular the surveillance of European citizens and politicians, undermined cooperation with the US over cybersecurity. The extent of the collaboration of Britain's GCHQ in US operations further damaged cooperation within the EU. Above all the Snowden revelations undermined the EU's confidence in US stewardship of the Internet. This has not been helped by the decision of the Trump administration to abandon the principle of net neutrality, without prior consultation with the EU. Although the EU and US jointly support the multi-stakeholder approach, their positions have never been fully aligned,[157] reflecting their different geopolitical conditions and cultures. The EU appears to be becoming increasingly frustrated with the US' unilateral approach to Internet governance. Cooper[158] admits that when post-modern states clash with modern states, the modern state is likely to come out on top. That may prove as true in cyber as in physical space. But more seriously, the EU's resentment of the US and the maverick nature of the Trump Administration is undermining the coherence of the "Free Internet Nations", increasing the chances that eventually the "Cyber Sovereignty Advocates" will win out.

The EU's problems in engaging in Cyberspace are complicated by the asymmetry between the EU's cyber capacities and those of individual member states, especially in cyber offence. All the other states looked at in this article have serious offensive cyber capabilities and are willing to use them. The EU as the EU does not. Offensive cyber capabilities, to the extent that they exist, exist at national level. But they do not exist equally across member states. Some states, such as the UK or France have serious offensive capabilities. Although Brexit may solve the problems that the NSA/GCHQ nexus poses for the EU, this asymmetry will remain with other member states, who are unlikely to be willing to share their capabilities with the EU or other member states on security grounds. To some extent this reflects the position in physical space, where the EU seeks to articulate a coherent Common Defence and Security Policy (CDSP), while real (if limited) military capabilities remain at national level and under national command. This may undermine the EU's ability as the EU to

157 http://www.egmontinstitute.be/content/uploads/2018/01/EPS-EU-cyber-partners_RENARD_AM.pdf?type=pdf.

158 Cooper: *The Breaking of Nations.*

participate effectively in bilateral or multilateral discussions of cybersecurity issues.

The frustrations that the EU has encountered in trying to promote its vision of Cyberspace, and possibly the implications of the Trump administration, may be producing a more aggressive assertion of the EU's normative diplomacy. The General Data Protection Regulation (GDPR), which came into effect in May of 2018, seeks to protect the privacy of the data of EU citizens. But its provisions, and protections, apply to the data of European citizens wherever that data is stored in the world. Any company, including foreign companies, that want to operate in the EU must accord the data of EU citizens the protections set out in the GDPR wherever they store it. In other words the EU is leveraging the attractiveness of its online market to establish the extraterritorial effect of the GDPR. In a sense it is classic EU normative diplomacy, but in a newly aggressive form. As the Irish Data Protection Commissioner, Helen Dixon, who takes the lead in ensuring the compliance with GDPR by the US Internet companies based there, has affirmed,[159] the EU is setting, and will impose, the data protection and privacy standards for the world. It seems unlikely that the Chinese will accept this. The EU risks a competition to see whose online market is more attractive.

As with the states we have looked at, the behaviour of the EU as the EU in cyberspace reflects the interaction of the EU's experience of cyberspace with its geopolitical culture, especially its self-image as a political model and norm setter. The geopolitical fields in which it operates are limited by its non-involvement in cyber offense at a Union level. The extent to which the Union's more aggressive attempts to establish cyberspace norms, eg on data protection, will be successful is questionable. It will depend on the attractiveness of the EU as an online market compared to other territories with different, or even contradictory, approaches to data protection. The key conflict may be between the GDPR and the Chinese Social Credit system (which requires the surrender of data about Chinese citizens to the Chinese Government). Internet companies (indeed all companies, given that all companies now collect data about customers and suppliers) will not welcome having to choose between operating in European or Chinese markets.

159 https://www.wired.co.uk/article/what-is-gdpr-uk-eu-legislation-compliance-summary-fines-2018.

21 Internet Companies

If it seemed strange to explore the European Union as a geopolitical actor, given that it was created to abolish geopolitics, it may seem even stranger to explore the role of Internet companies as geopolitical actors. But there is nothing new in the geopolitics of companies. From the 17th to 19th centuries the British East India Company was a major geopolitical actor, possessed of its own armies and navies and administering India as a British colony. In the 20th century the "seven sisters", the major western oil companies, were major geopolitical actors, effectively running countries and enjoying the military and political support of their home countries. It can even be argued that major US fruit companies served as geopolitical actors in Latin American politics. Given the development and importance of Cyberspace, it should not therefore be surprising that Internet companies should become the 21st century equivalents of the "seven sisters", even if that is not how the companies see it themselves. This section will explore two kinds of Internet company: search engines like Google; and social media platforms like Twitter, Facebook and YouTube. This is not to underestimate the importance of other Internet companies like Amazon and Apple. But these two categories play a particular role in conflict in Cyberspace.

21.1 *Algorithms*

The key to the geopolitical role of search engines and social media platforms in Cyberspace is the algorithms that underlie them. The algorithms play different roles, but in both categories they shape the geography of Cyberspace for certain activities, both in the sense of deciding what data arrives where, and in placing limits on the reach of individual actors. In the case of search engines like Google, the algorithms decide in what order the results of an individual search are presented to the user. Given that most users do not look beyond the first page of Google results, this is important if a web content designer wants to secure high profile for their content. By studying how Google operates, it is possible to identify key criteria which decide which web-pages will get priority in a search. These are known as Search Engine Optimisation (SEO) techniques. They are invaluable for e-commerce companies, journalists or politicians who want to ensure that their web content secures profile and makes an impact. But they can also be manipulated by malicious actors to ensure profile is given in searches to disinformation or provocative content. For example, in late 2016 a search in Google for "Did the holocaust happen?" generated a series of webpages by holocaust denial and neo-Nazi groups.[160] It took Google some time to take down the holocaust denial sites, in part because it was reluctant to alter its search algorithms (or give away too many secrets about them). This case may have produced more embarrassment than real damage, but it demonstrates the scope for malicious actors to use search engines to give profile to disinformation in an attempt to distort public debate and destabilise democratic societies. The danger is even greater with the development of "Deepfake" techniques, in which a combination of machine learning and video techniques are used to generate videos in which people appear credibly to be saying things that they have not said (and would not say).[161] While these techniques are still at an early stage of development, and some of the fake videos produced relatively easy to spot, they are improving rapidly. The dangers are not hard to foresee. The UAE orchestrated hack of Qatar Government systems in 2017 resulted in the posting of inflammatory comments attributed to the Emir of Qatar.[162] These "fake statements" were sufficient to justify a Saudi led blockade of Qatar (and secure the support of President Trump). Had the UAE orchestrated hackers been able also to post a "deepfake" video of the Emir apparently making the statements in person, the impact would have been even more immediate, and potentially more dangerous.

Algorithms function differently in social media platforms. There they aim at ensuring the user receives content that he or she is likely to enjoy, be pleased with or interested in. Initially this begins by suggesting contacts or friends that are likely to appeal to the user, to help him or her extend their social network. It then extends to content, and most importantly, to adverts tailored to the interests or tastes of the user. This essentially is how the social media platforms are able to finance themselves. However, the problem is that the same algorithms that drive the tailored marketing, also ensure that the user only receives the news and opinions that he or she is likely to like or agree with. Social media did not create the echo chambers which are undermining social and political narratives in western societies, but they are reinforcing them.[163] More seriously, like search engines, they can be used to spread disinformation and fake news, in efforts to influence and undermine western political debates.

160 https://www.theguardian.com/commentisfree/2016/dec/11/google-frames-shapes-and-distorts-how-we-see-world.

161 https://www.youtube.com/watch?v=cQ54GDm1eLo.

162 https://www.washingtonpost.com/world/national-security/uae-hacked-qatari-Government-sites-sparking-regional-upheaval-according-to-us-intelligence-officials/2017/07/16/00c46e54-698f-11e7-8eb5-cbccc2e7bfbf_story.html?noredirect=on&utm_term=.d5a1c24e2204.

163 https://www.uscpublicdiplomacy.org/blog/really-dark-side-facebook.

In a sense the role of social media algorithms is even more pernicious than that of search engines. The algorithms underlying social media do not only spread disinformation. They also ensure that it arrives in the echo chambers most likely to believe, where it fits in with the pre-existing prejudices of the members of the echo chamber. Once again the evolution of "Deepfake" technologies worsens the problems.

21.2 *Internet Companies' Experience of Cyberspace*

Internet companies experienced Cyberspace very differently from the other actors examined in this article. Firstly, the Internet already existed before their creation. Unlike the US, they were not instrumental in creating the Internet. Unlike Russia or China, they did not experience the Internet as a foreign imposition or an existential threat. Rather it was something in which they developed, and without which they could not exist. Since their invention, both search engines and social media platforms have gone through various phases. The first phase is what might be called the idealistic phase, captured by Google's motto "Don't be evil" (subsequently adapted during Google's restructuring as Alphabet to "Do the right thing"). The Internet companies saw themselves as new kinds of entities pursuing moral paths, as forces for good in the world. As they became ever wealthier, the moral aspects were undermined. Google's initial refusal to collaborate with Chinese Government censorship had broken down by 2018, as it agreed to develop a special search machine for China (the consternation of many of its own workers appears to have forced Google to abandon the Dragonfly project at the end of 2018[164]). Facebook found itself caught up in a series of scandals about the use it allowed to be made of its users' data. The Cambridge Analytica scandal, which revealed that Facebook had allowed Cambridge Analytica to use applications to gather Facebook users' data to allow more targeted campaigning in the US elections.[165] These problems and scandals marked a second phase in the Internet companies' experience of Cyberspace, where they moved from being forces for good to being seen by the public, and reluctantly by themselves, as mechanisms for monetising the data of their users. This move provoked growing concerns among the public and Government, in particular in western Europe, about the use and protection of citizens' data. As noted in the previous section, this culminated in the EU's GDPR. However, the Internet companies are still

---

164 https://www.thetimes.co.uk/article/google-abandons-censored-search-engine-for-china-zpjhxlzro.

165 https://www.theguardian.com/uk-news/2018/mar/22/cambridge-analytica-scandal-the-biggest-revelations-so-far.

unwilling, or unable, to accept or assimilate the third phase of their experience of Cyberspace: as active players in geopolitical conflict in Cyberspace.

21.3 *Internet Companies and Information Operations*

Given the ability of the algorithms underlying social media to ensure that disinformation and fake news gets to the echo chambers already predisposed to believe it, it is unsurprising that those using information warfare techniques to undermine the political and social stability of western societies would take advantage of them. This article has already discussed Russia's preference for cyber disinformation and disruption operations to destabilise the US and European countries. There is now considerable evidence[166] that Russian operatives, working directly for Russian intelligence agencies or indirectly as controlled surrogates, made extensive use of Facebook, Twitter and other social media to try to influence the 2016 Brexit vote and the US Presidential elections the same year, as well as elections in France and Germany. It is not simply that the social media platforms are being taken advantage of by countries launching disinformation and disruption operations. The very design of the algorithms underlying them gives an asymmetric advantage to the disinformation operations. Three key features of disinformation and disruption operations explain this: they are not aimed at convincing those that do not agree with them, but rather at undermining confidence in all narratives; they are not overt, in the sense that the Government behind them does not openly own up to the operations, often hiding its role behind surrogates; because of the previous two points, they do not have to be coherent, but can segment their messages to appeal to different echo chambers. The Western public diplomacy response is different: it does seek to convince people; it has to do so because it is overt, in the sense that the Governments behind it admit to it; and therefore it must be coherent to be convincing. Disinformation and disruption operations can segment their messages and fake news to appeal to different (often opposed) echo chambers, while relying on the social media algorithms to deliver them to the echo chambers predisposed to believe them. But the same social media algorithms will ensure that coherent western public diplomacy messages will reach only those who already agree with them. In short, social media algorithms facilitate disinformation and disruption operations, but frustrate public diplomacy.

But the social media companies are reluctant to accept the extent of the problem, or the proactive role played by their algorithms. Facebook is a case in point. Reluctantly, under pressure from western Governments and media, Facebook has agreed to take down pages thought to be used by Russian intelligence

166 Singer: *LikeWar*.

officers or bots. But it remains unwilling to share details of its algorithms with western Governments. It portrays itself as a neutral platform which Russians and others are taking advantage of. But it may not understand the concept of neutrality in Cyberspace. Neutrality in physical space carries both privileges and obligations, and cannot always be maintained. One obligation is that a neutral country shall not allow another country's armed forces to cross its territory to attack a third country. As discussed above, in 1914 Belgium's neutrality had been guaranteed by the 1830 treaty which had created the country. When the German Government requested passage across Belgian territory for its troops to attack France, the Belgian Government was faced with a difficult choice. If it acquiesced to the German request, it breached its neutrality obligations and became a de facto ally of Germany. If it refused the request and resisted the German advance, it became a de facto ally of France against Germany. It chose the latter and paid a terrible price. Ironically, and as indicted above, it is difficult to see how this provision of neutrality could apply to countries in Cyberspace. As Libicki points out,[167] given the way that the Internet works splitting up packets of information and re-assembling them at their destination, it is virtually impossible for Governments to be aware of all the information passing through the optic fibre cables passing through their country. It would therefore be most unreasonable to hold them responsible for data passing through the cables on their territory as part of a cyber attack on a third country. However, the provision can be applied to social media companies. Either they allow disinformation operations to continue on their platforms, in which case they become de facto allies of those carrying out the operations (most recently Russia). Or they collaborate fully with western Governments (eg by sharing details about their algorithms with western Governments), in which case they become de facto allies of the west against Russia and other disrupters. This latter, of course, runs a similar risk as that run by Belgium: by siding fully with the west they negate their usefulness for Russian disinformation operations and may themselves become targets for disruption and degeneration attacks.

The social media platforms are reluctant to see it like this, not least because they are reluctant to share details about their algorithms. These algorithms are their competitive advantage and drive their incomes from advertising. They are reluctant to share them with Governments, concerned that the details could leak. Thus we have geopolitical actors who refuse to see themselves as such because of the implications for their business models. But just as they have become embroiled in arguments about data protection, they will

---

167 Libicki: *Cyberspace in Peace and War*.

inevitably get drawn further into debates about their role in disinformation campaigns. Even if search engines and social media platforms do not want to see themselves as geopolitical actors, they do play a key role in shaping the Cyberspace environment, and its geography, where some forms of cyberconflict take place.

By the same token, we can apply a critical geopolitics approach to internet companies operating in Cyberspace. Their experience of Cyberspace (geopolitical condition) is of something normal. For them Cyberspace is the essential domain in which they operate. Without it they do not exist. The geopolitical field in which they operate initially centred on information gathering or building social networks. Unlike the states we have looked at, they do not have a geopolitical culture that precedes, or is separate from, their engagement with Cyberspace. Their geopolitical culture derives from their engagement with Cyberspace. Thus deriving from their initial geopolitical field, spreading information and promoting social interaction online, it is positive, seeing them as almost altruistic operators in Cyberspace. Only slowly as the geopolitical fields in which they operated shifted to commercial marketing and the monetising of their users' data did their geopolitical culture have to accept the commercial element, but still along-side their self-image as a force for good. They still have not been able to assimilate the implications of the final geopolitical field in which they operate, the battlefield for information conflict between, primarily, Russia and the West. From the point of view of geopolitical culture, they remain in denial (perhaps analogous to the kind of self-denial generated by US exceptionalism).

22 The Implications for Diplomacy and Foreign Policy

Diplomacy's engagement with Cyberspace so far has been largely limited to the use of digital technologies, and within that to the use of social media platforms. There has been some interesting work on how digital technologies can support consular work. But the main focus, of both practitioners and scholars, has been on the use of social media platforms.[168] The story has not been a happy one. Foreign Ministries have seen social media as a way to do public diplomacy on the cheap. Foreign Ministry and Embassy social media campaigns have been understaffed. Diplomats, and some scholars, have failed to understand the impact of underlying algorithms, limiting the reach of social

---

168 Corneliu Bjola and Marcus Holmes (ed): *Digital Diplomacy Theory and Practice*, Routledge, 2015.

media based public diplomacy to those who already agree (as explored above). Hierarchical structures and a reluctance to delegate authority to participate in social media debates to embassies and individual diplomats has undermined their credibility and effectiveness. Too much social media based public diplomacy has reverted to one way messaging, rather than the genuine engagement with foreign publics that was beginning to emerge: a backward step. But at least there has been debate, and there is a growing realisation of the challenges and pitfalls of depending too much on social media.

In as far as diplomacy has engaged with Cyberspace as an arena of activity (rather than a provider of technology) it has largely limited itself to Internet governance issues, including dealing with cybercrime.[169] Even much of this has been left to technicians or other experts. Internet governance is not seen by most countries as a major foreign policy issue. As explored above, Internet governance in the European Union is dealt with primarily by the European Commission, whose technical experts deal both with negotiations about cybercrime and Internet governance. Member states seem happy to leave these issues to the Commission in a way that they would not be happy to leave other foreign policy issues. And yet, as explored above, this is not how countries like Russia and China see these issues. For both countries, Internet governance is a central part of their foreign policy, conditioned by the way they have experienced Cyberspace and their geopolitical cultures.

Diplomats and diplomacy seem to have engaged even less with the broader cybersecurity issues. In part this may be the result of careless use of language. The constant referral to cyberattacks, without distinguishing between different types of operations and the motivations that drive them, encourage both the tendency for all "hostile" cyber operators to be lumped together, as well as the tendency to believe that there is little that diplomacy can do about this, and it is best left to technicians and the military. It is interesting that cybersecurity tends to be far more prominent in national defence or security strategies than in foreign policy documents. There seems to be a feeling that technicians created the Internet, and technicians can come up with technical solutions to its problems. If not, they should be passed to the military or the intelligence services. But as shown earlier in this article, many of these problems are highly political or geopolitical. Leaving them to technicians and the military is akin to leaving all international security issues in physical space to the military. This is not to denigrate the military, but, as Kortunov argues,[170] diplomats

169 https://www.diplomacy.edu/sites/default/files/Policy_papers_briefs_09_JK.pdf.

170 http://russiancouncil.ru/en/analytics-and-comments/analytics/politics-as-continuation-of-war-by-other-means/.

bring a different and valuable perspective. Technical and security solutions in Cyberspace are necessary, but they are not sufficient.

The point is made by the recent controversy about the Chinese company Huawei's involvement in setting industrial standards for 5G telephony, as discussed above. For years the Chinese only sent small delegations to industry standard setting meetings, while the West left participation in such meetings to technicians and technical experts from Government and industry. Such technical experts did not appreciate the significance of the sudden increase in the size of Chinese delegations at these meetings, or the security and geopolitical implications of Huawei's involvement in setting industrial standards and developing technologies for 5G. As we have seen, by the time the US Government realised what had happened it was reduced to a difficult fight to recover "lost territory". Had diplomats been present from the beginning they would have been better placed to realise the implications and head off problems at an earlier stage.[171]

This reflects a broader trend in western, especially European, diplomacy since the 1990s. As evident in the discussion of the EU, globalisation and the apparent global convergence led diplomats to focus on the global issues, or new international security, agenda. More traditional geopolitical agendas focused on territory, resources, inter-state conflict, spheres of influence and the balance of power were thought consigned to the dustbin of history. Interstate rivalry would now be fought out through commercial competition. Diplomatic services and embassies, especially in Europe, were largely reconfigured to focus on global issues and commercial promotion (which became their major justification at a time of budget cuts). The re-emergence of more geopolitical agendas with the Russian invasion of Georgia in 2008 and annexation of the Crimea in 2014[172] and the projection of Chinese sovereignty into the South China Sea[173] came as an unpleasant surprise. But historians may judge that in fact the geopolitics never went away. The illusion of political as well as economic globalisation and the convergence of values was generated by US geopolitical domination following the end of the Cold War. As Kagan put it,[174] "The World has become normal again".

The preliminary analysis of the geopolitics of Cyberspace in this article suggests that diplomats and diplomacy need to engage more deeply in Cyberspace,

171 http://thecorner.eu/world-economy/5g-the-real-reason-behind-us-attacks-on-huawei/78010/.

172 Toal: *Near Abroad.*

173 Kerry Brown: *What Does China Want? China's World,* I B Tauris, 2017.

174 Robert Kagan: *The Return of History and the Endo f Dreams,* Atlantic Books, 2008.

and in particular with cybersecurity. Cybersecurity issues should move to the centre of foreign policy, rather than being left to national defence or security. Diplomats can bring a range of techniques and ways of seeing the world that can help bring greater stability to Cyberspace. As we have seen with 5G and Huawei, leaving Internet governance to domestic ministries and technicians risks the geopolitical aspects being overlooked. Leaving cybersecurity to technicians, the military and intelligence services risks escalation in intelligence operations, especially as the latter two groups will tend to see solutions in terms of responses in Cyberspace rather than conversations in physical space. As the old saw has it, if your only tool is a hammer, everything looks like a nail. Valeriano et al[175] argues that there have been few degeneration attacks with Kinetic effect (one definite and one possible[176]) and that the risks of escalation may have been exaggerated. But the use of Cyberspace for degeneration, disruption and information operations is at an early stage. It is too early to assess the risks of escalation, especially, as Buchanan argues,[177] cyber operations pose particular problems of intention identification and attribution. Diplomats are needed to help manage this and other issues emerging in Cyberspace.

This raises the issue of what diplomacy and diplomats can bring to the party. The author explores this in detail elsewhere.[178] This article will indicate some of the key areas where diplomacy can contribute to generating stability in Cyberspace. A key diplomatic skill is empathy, the ability to see a problem through the eyes of the other, or even a rival (this is a skill that frequently results in diplomats being unfairly accused of "going native" – representing the foreign Government rather than her own). The geopolitical analysis in this article has sought to show how the behaviour of different international actors in Cyberspace has been shaped by the way they have experienced Cyberspace and the country's geopolitical culture. As Valeriano et al[179] suggest this is essential in identifying the kind of operations a country will carry out, and the motivations behind these operations. This kind of diplomacy used to be central to the work of political officer diplomats, as shown by Kennan's famous long telegram[180] from the US embassy in Moscow in 1946, which helped shape the US' containment strategy during the Cold War. Diplomats need to recover this capability for engaging with Cyberspace (not to mention physical space). It will be key not only in anticipating the behaviour of major players in

175 Valeriano et al: *Cyber Strategy.*
176 Sanger: *The Perfect Weapon.*
177 Buchanan: *The Cybersecurity Dilemma.*
178 Shaun Riordan: *Cyberdiplomacy: Managing Security and Governance Online.*
179 Valeriano et al: *Cyber Strategy.*
180 John Lewis Gaddis: *George F Kennan: An American Life*, Penguin, 2012.

Cyberspace, but also in identifying areas of possible cooperation, or common areas on which future agreements can be constructed.

Sharp[181] argues that diplomats form an international community of diplomats, with common norms, attitudes and ways of seeing the world. In part this reflects the alienation of diplomats both from the citizens of the country where they are posted and from their own fellow nationals. In some senses diplomats have more in common with each other than with their fellow nationals. This commonality of experience facilitates the ability of diplomats to manage international affairs. They can, example, keep the conversation going with diplomats of other countries in circumstances (eg conflict) where politicians cannot. Sharp highlights the important role of socialisation into this international community of diplomats. He cites the example of Soviet diplomats, who immediately after the Russian revolution are sent abroad to provoke revolution, but who by the 1930s have been socialised as "normal" members of the international diplomatic community. A challenge for diplomats will be to construct an international community of diplomats in Cyberspace promoting stability and managing cybersecurity issues. It may be objected that this will not be able to include non-state actors. However, this is true also of physical space, where it is difficult to conceive of ISIS ever being socialised into the international community. However, this objection may be less important than it appears. The image of the lone hacker creating severe kinetic damage by hacking into critical infrastructure may be more illusion than reality. All the cyber degeneration operations and the vast majority of cyber disruption, cyberespionage and cyber disinformation operations have been carried out by Government agencies or surrogates acting on their instigation (whether "patriotic hackers" or criminal hacking groups).[182] Indeed the close relations between the Russian Government and organised cyber criminal gangs (the "siloviki-organised crime symbiosis") means that socialising Russia within an international cyber community (if possible) could bring additional benefits in fighting cyber crime.

Diplomats take a variety of approaches to international law, ranging from the highly juridical approach of some European diplomats, via the more pragmatic view of Anglo-Saxon diplomats to the rejection of existing international law as a hypocritical western imposition by some Asian countries (and on occasion Russia). There is no clear position on whether existing international law applies to Cyberspace. The EU affirms in its Cyberstrategy that it does. But both Russia and China have rowed back from apparent commitments to the same effect given in early meetings of the UN Group of Government Experts

181 Paul Sharp: *Diplomatic Theory of Diplomatic Relations*, Cambridge University Press, 2009.

182 Klimburg: *The Darkening Web*.

(GEE).[183] In fact, existing international law, designed for physical space, does not translate easily into Cyberspace. Libicki[184] points out that the concept of neutrality is problematic in Cyberspace (as this article argued in the context of Internet companies). Negotiations to limit weapon types or numbers make little sense in Cyberspace, whereas negotiations to limit targets, especially for kinetic attack, do (eg putting critical civilian infrastructure off limits). Critics may argue that establishing international norms of behaviour in Cyberspace will have little value, given the ease of concealment and the problems of attribution. But they may be missing the point. International Law in physical space is as much honoured in the breach as in the observance. The English school of international relations argues that this is less important than a country's image of itself as a member of the international community and an observer of international law[185] (the same point as made by Nye about normative taboos in the context of deterrence[186]). Governments do not ask themselves what are their options under international law in any given situation. Rather they decide on a course of action in accordance with their interests, and then ask how they can make this course of action appear to be in accordance with international law. This remains an effective constraint on international behaviour because there are some courses of action that cannot be made to appear to be in accordance with international law, and are therefore ruled out for countries which want to remain members of the international community.[187] A similar approach to international law, or norms, may have to be adopted in Cyberspace, emphasising the importance of both the empathetic analysis of geopolitical conditions and culture, and the socialisation of key actors into an international community of cyber actors.

In negotiating agreements on cybersecurity and, even more so, engaging with the Internet governance agenda diplomats will have to engage with a broad range of non-state actors. This requires developing a greater capacity for multi-stakeholder diplomacy: the capacity to interact with a range of state and non-state actors, and to form heterogenous coalitions built on shared preferred outcomes rather than shared values or ideologies. This has already been true of the global issues or new international security agenda, where diplomats have to engage and negotiate with a broad range of companies, NGOs and civil society groups. The same will be true of the Internet governance agenda, where

183 Segal: *The Hacked World Order.*
184 Libicki: *Cyberspace in Peace and War.*
185 Buzan: *An Introduction to the English School of International Relations.*
186 Nye: *Deterrence and Dissuasion in Cyberspace.*
187 Riordan: *Cyberdiplomacy.*

agreements may proceed through bottom up global networks of state and non-state actors, along the lines of the Paris Accords on climate change[160]. There are dangers here for diplomats and diplomacy. Just as diplomats may seek to socialise international actors into the international community of diplomats, so other non-state actors may socialise diplomats into their own world views, whether that of the NGO or the major corporation. The risk is that the diplomat who, through multi-stakeholder diplomacy, is socialised into the ethical world view of the NGO may no longer be able to play her role as a diplomat.

The major novelty in Cyberspace is the extent to which multi-stakeholder diplomacy is relevant to the cybersecurity agenda. Although, for now, the key players in the international cybersecurity agenda continue to be states and their surrogates, there is a further category of non-Governmental actor with which diplomats will increasingly need to deal: the Internet companies, and especially those associated with search engines and social media platforms. As this article has argued, whether they like it or not, these Internet companies are geopolitical actors in their own right, and need to be treated as such. The Danish Government has appointed Caspar Klynge as Ambassador to the Tech sector.[188] Other countries have followed suit. His role includes:

- Gathering information on new and future technological developments and analysing their impact on diplomacy, politics and Danish society;
- Gathering information on developments within the technological sector itself, relations between tech companies and their plans for future operations/investments;
- Discussing ethical and regulatory issues with technological companies, with a focus on unacceptable content and data and privacy protection;
- Convincing technology companies to base operations, research facilities or European subsidiaries in Denmark;
- Promoting Denmark as a highly digitalised country at the cutting edge of new technologies and thinking (Klynge's appointment as Denmark's Tech Ambassador itself contributes to this).

This looks very much like any bilateral embassy: information gathering, discussing regulatory issues, representation, public diplomacy and commercial promotion. The one element missing from a bilateral embassy is engaging the host as a geopolitical actor. This may have to be the next step for tech ambassadors, engaging with Internet companies as geopolitical actors, and spelling out to them the legal and political consequences of their actions, or inaction.

A further implication for diplomacy relates to cyber disinformation and disruption operations. As this article has argued, the algorithms underlying the

188 http://techamb.um.dk/.

social media on which public diplomacy has increasingly depended limit the effectiveness of that public diplomacy, while at the same time facilitating the disinformation and disruption operations. Diplomats may need to revert to older forms of more targeted diplomacy. Social media have to some extent made diplomats lazy, creating the illusion that they allow diplomats' to reach out to the whole public by tweeting or posting on Facebook. As this article has argued, in fact they are likely to limit the public diplomacy to those who already agree with it. This is equally true with strategic communication, which amounts to one way messaging, in itself lacking credibility, being directed by the algorithms to those who already doubt the fake news or disinformation. An earlier, pre-social media, form of public diplomacy identified key opinion formers, whom it then cultivated and sought to influence as a way of influencing foreign public opinions indirectly. A key challenge for this kind of public diplomacy was finding ways of engaging with and influencing hostile opinion formers. Combating cyber disinformation and disruption operations, in a world of echo chambers reinforced by social media algorithms, will require diplomats, and policy makers, to revert to this earlier form of public diplomacy, using the targeting and cultivation of individual influential opinion formers to bridge across the different echo chambers.

A final point relates to the way in which digital technologies have accelerated the speed of events and, even more, the speed at which they are reported and debated in social media. Technologies in the pipeline such as AI, machine learning and quantum computing will only reinforce this trend. This will force diplomatic services to re-think the way in which they are structured, and in particular the way in which embassies abroad relate to their Foreign Ministries. Effective engagement with social media already requires Foreign Ministries to delegate authority to diplomats abroad to participate in social media debates – there is simply not time to refer back to headquarters for instructions (the fact that most Foreign Ministries remain reluctant to delegate such authority means that most digital diplomacy is, by definition, ineffective). But the acceleration of events and information flows may force Foreign Ministries into a broader delegation of authority to embassies and ambassadors. In the future Foreign Ministries may be limited to setting the objectives of the diplomatic mission, leaving it up to the diplomats on the ground how to achieve them. In the military this is known as mission command or Auftragstaktik.[189] Ironically, the needs of Cyberspace may make Ambassadors truly plenipotentiary again.

189 Eitan Shamir: *Transforming Command: The Pursuit of Mission Command in the US, British and Israeli Armies*, Stanford, 2011.

23 Conclusion

This is only an initial attempt to apply geopolitical analysis to Cyberspace on a limited number of actors. It would be interesting to see whether this kind of approach, whether using classical or critical geopolitics, could be applied to other countries and types of actors. Nevertheless, some preliminary conclusions can be drawn. Both classical and critical geopolitics can be applied to Cyberspace and can generate some interesting insights. The physical infrastructure underlying the Internet as well as the network cyber structures act as the geography of Cyberspace and shape how the actors, including state actors, interact. The way in which state actors experience Cyberspace (geopolitical conditions) combines with their geopolitical culture to shape how they behave in the different geopolitical fields in Cyberspace where they operate.

It is important to be more discriminating in the use of terminology in relation to Cyberspace. Lumping all cyber operations together as cyberattacks misses out on the distinctions between different types of cyber operations, as well as conditioning perceptions and reactions. A cyber attack is something that must be responded to. A cyber operation less so. It is interesting that in physical space one would not normally talk about an espionage "attack", whereas in Cyberspace it is common to talk about a cyberespionage attack. Using more neutral terms like cyber operations, and then distinguishing between them according to objectives and motivations, avoids prejudicing the analysis and conditioning responses.

Different countries carry out different kinds of cyber operations for different reasons. Not all "bad actors" carry out the same kind of operations for the same reasons. Russia focuses heavily on cyber disruption and disinformation operations. Even when it carries out a cyberespionage operation, it is often in support of a subsequent disinformation or disruption operation (eg hacking the DNC computers so the data stolen could then be released through Wikileaks). In contrast, China focuses on cyberespionage primarily to help close a perceived technology gap, and is less interested in cyber disruption. Valeriano et al[190] try to capture this by dividing states into status quo states (who prefer enforcement operations), rising states (who prefer espionage operations) and declining states (who prefer disruption operations). There seems to be some truth in this from the examples this article looked at (although it is not clear if Russia is a declining power compared, for example, with where it was in 1995, or even 2008). However, the critical geopolitical analysis seems to give a richer and more nuanced account of why states behave in different ways. State

190 Valeriano et al: *Cyber Strategy*.

behaviour and motivation can also be dynamic over time. Once China has closed the technology gap it may have less interest in cyberespionage operations, or even be concerned about being the victim of such operations (this may have lain behind the 2015 agreement between Xi and Obama). Indeed, as China further integrates its economy into the Internet, and increases its vulnerability to cyber operations of all kinds, it may become a potential ally against cyber disrupters like Russia, N. Korea or Iran.

Internet companies, and especially those associated with search engines and social media platforms, are geopolitical actors whether they like it or not. They shape the environment in which cyber operations take place. In a sense they are the geopolitical fields in which disruption and disinformation campaigns play out. Their claims to be neutral platforms are not credible, and demonstrate the limitations of the concept of neutrality in Cyberspace. The Danish appointment, followed by others, of an Ambassador to the technology sector (Tech Ambassador) is an interesting initiative, although most of his activities fall outside the purview of this article. But in the future role of a Tech Ambassador may have to include spelling out the geopolitical realities to Internet companies, and pressuring them into greater collaboration.

Diplomats and Foreign Ministries need to engage more effectively in Cyberspace, and not just in the sense of identifying tools to use to advance their broader diplomatic agendas. Cyberspace is now one of the key domains where diplomats must operate. Diplomats need to develop further multiple-stakeholder skills to enable them to engage effectively in the Internet governance debates. In doing so they should beware being "socialised" into NGO or civil society mindsets which could undermine their ability to perform their diplomatic role. In tackling the cybersecurity agenda, they should draw on the kind of critical geopolitical analysis explored in this article not just to understand better the motivations of different state and non-state actors, and anticipate the kinds of operations they might launch, but also to identify possible areas of common interests or shared preferred outcomes which can serve as the basis for the construction of a series of norms of behaviour in Cyberspace. The aim should be to construct an international community in Cyberspace, and then socialise the various actors into becoming part of it. Ironically, Cyberspace may need modern versions of very traditional diplomatic activities.

Diplomats and Foreign Ministries also need to give greater thought to the consequences of new technologies for their culture and structures. This remains an under investigated area. One consequence of digital technologies has been the acceleration in the speed of events and a reduction of reaction times. This not only means that traditional hierarchical structures no longer cut the mustard, but that diplomats in the field do not have time to seek instructions from capital cities before they have to react (feel for the poor US diplomats having to respond in real time to President Trump's late night Twitter storms). Governments and Foreign Ministries may have to delegate more power and authority to their overseas missions. Ambassadors may become plenipotentiary again.

Bibliography

Ball, Phillip. *Critical Mass: How One Thing Leads to Another*, Arrow, 2005.

Baños, Pedro. *How They Rule the World*, Random House, 2019.

Barabasi, Albert-Laszlo. *Linked: The New Science of Networks*, Perseus, 2003.

Bjola, Corneliu and Marcus Holmes (eds.). *Digital Diplomacy Theory and Practice*, Routledge, 2015.

Brands, Hal. *Making the Unipolar Moment: US Foreign Policy and the Rise of the Post-Cold War Order*, Cornell, 2016.

Bremmer, Ian. *The End of the Freemarket: Who Wins the War between States and Corporations?*, Viking, 2010.

Brown, Kerry. *CEO, China: The Rise of Xi Jinping*, I B Tauris, 2017.

Brown, Kerry. *What Does China Want? China's World*, I B Tauris, 2017.

Buchanan, Ben. *The Cybersecurity Dilemma: Network Intrusions, Trust and Fear in the International System*, C. Hurst & Co, 2017.

Buzan, Barry. *An Introduction to the English School of International Relations*, Polity, 2014.

Choucri, Nazli. *Cyberpolitics in International Relations*, MIT Press, 2012.

Clover, Charles. *Black Wind, White Snow: The Rise of Russia's New Nationalism*, Yale University Press, 2017.

Cooper, Robert. *The Breaking of Nations: Order and Chaos in the Twenty-First Century*, Atlantic Books, 2003.

Dittmer, Jason. *Diplomatic Material: Affect, Assemblage and Foreign Policy*, Duke University Press, 2017.

Dodds, Klaus. *Geopolitics: A Very Short Introduction*, Oxford University Press, 2014.

Friedman, George. *The Next 100 Years: A Forecast for the 21st Century*, Allison & Busby, 2010.

Fukuyama, Francis. *The End of History and the Last Man*, Simon and Schuster, 2006.

Gaddis, John Lewis. *George F Kennan: An American Life*, Penguin, 2012.

Galeotti, Mark. *The Vory: Russia's Super Mafia*, Yale University Press, 2018.

Guehenno, Jean-Marie. *The End of the Nation State*, University of Minnesota Press, 2000.

Harding, Luke. *The Snowden Files: The Inside Story of the World's Most Wanted Man*, Guardian Faber, 2014.
Herwig, Holger H. *The Demon of Geopolitics: How Karl Haushofer "Educated" Hitler and Hess*, Rowan and Littlefield, 2016.
Kagan, Robert. *The Return of History and the End of Dreams*, Atlantic Books, 2008.
Kaplan, Fred. *Dark Territory: The Secret History of Cyber War*, Simon & Schuster, 2016.
Kello, Lucas. *The Virtual Weapon and International Order*, Yale, 2017.
Kershaw, Ian. *Hitler 1936-1945: Nemesis*, Allen Lane, 2001.
Khanna, Parag. *Connectography: Mapping the Global Network Revolution*, W&N, 2017.
Kissinger, Henry. *Diplomacy*, Simon and Schuster, 1994.
Kissinger, Henry. *On China*, Penguin, 2011.
Klimburg, Alexander. *The Darkening Web: The War for Cyberspace*, Penguin, 2017.
Libicki, Martin C. *Cyberspace in Peace and War*, Naval Institute Press, 2016.
Marshall, Tim. *Prisoners of Geography*, Elliot and Thompson, 2016.
Murphy, David T. *The Heroic Earth: Geopolitical Thought in Weimar Germany, 1918–1933*, Kent State University, 1997.
Pantsov, Alexander V. *Deng Xiaoping: A Revolutionary Life*, Oxford University Press, 2017.
Patrikarakos, David. *War in 140 Characters: How Social Media Is Reshaping Conflict In The Twenty-First Century*, Basic Books, 2017.
Payne, Kenneth. *Strategy Evolution And War: From Apes to Artificial Intelligence*, Georgetown University Press, 2018.
Perez Martinez, Jorge and Zoraida Frias Barroso. *A Level Playing Field for the Digital Ecosystem*, Telefónica, 2016.
Perkovich, George and Ariel E. Levite (eds.). *Understanding Cyber Conflict: 14 Analogies*, Georgetown University Press, 2017.
Riordan, Shaun. *Cyberdiplomacy: Managing Security and Governance Online*, Polity, 2019.
Sanger, David. *The Perfect Weapon: Sabotage and Fear in the Cyber Age*, Scribe UK, 2018.
Segal, Adam. *The Hacked World Order: How Nations Fight, Trade, Maneuver and Manipulate in the Digital Age*, Public Affairs, 2017.
Shamir, Eitan. *Transforming Command: The Pursuit of Mission Command in the US, British and Israeli Armies*, Yale, 2011.
Sharp, Paul. *Diplomatic Theory of Diplomatic Relations*, Cambridge University Press, 2009.
Singer, P. W. *LikeWar: The Weaponisation of Social Media*, Eamon Dolan/Houghton Mifflin Harcourt, 2018.
Soldatov, Andrei and Irina Borogan. *Red Web: The Kremlin's Wars on the Internet*, Public Affairs, 2017.

Spykman, Nicholas J. *America's Strategy in World Politics: The United States and the Balance of Power*, Transaction Publishers, 2007.
Tal, Mikhail. *The Life and Games of Mikhail Tal*, Everyman Chess, 1997.
Thucydides. *The History of the Peloponnesian War*, Penguin, 2000.
Toal, Gerard. *Near Abroad: Putin, the West, and the Contest over Ukraine and the Caucasus*, Oxford University Press, 2017.
Valeriano, Brandon, Benjamin Jensen and Ryan C. Maness. *Cyber Strategy: The Evolving Character of Power and Coercion*, Oxford University Press, 2018.

Author Biography

Shaun Riordan (MA Hons, Cambridge 1983) is Director of the Chair for Diplomacy and Cyberspace at the European Institute for International Studies and a Senior Visiting Fellow of the Clingendael Institute. A former British diplomat, he is author of *The New Diplomacy* (Polity 2003) and *Cyberdiplomacy: Managing Security and Governance Online* (Polity 2019).

www.ingramcontent.com/pod-product-compliance
Lightning Source LLC
Chambersburg PA
CBHW031332230926
51848CB00001B/198
9789004409361